# WORDS
# OF
# WATER

Reverend
Prince Kojo
Essiem

# WORDS OF WATER CHAPTERS

# PREFACE

My heart is to continue the work of my Lord Jesus Christ. If you are behind the walls of a prison of this world, no matter its design or structure: sickness, poverty, unemployment, prejudice, addiction, or anything else, there is a message of freedom within these pages! These sermon summaries are designed to help you come to know and experience the following:

## GOD LOVES YOU!

- ➢ **Jesus has paid your sin debt for you for free – simply accept it and it is yours**
- ➢ **Evil has no power over you if you have accepted Jesus**
- ➢ **You walk in God's favor once you realize you are adopted into a family of believers**

The Holy Spirit continues to give me messages to share with those He wants to hear. No matter where you are in life, physically, emotionally, mentally, and spiritually, there is a message just for you inside this volume. Open your heart today and be blessed. And know that I love you and will be praying for you as well.

By His grace,

*Rev. Prince Kojo Essiem*

Rev. Prince Kojo Essiem

# REV. PRINCE KOJO ESSIEM

## Biography

Rev. Prince Kojo Essiem is the General Overseer of Divine Power Ministry (DivinePowerMinistry.org) and the Head Pastor of the headquarters location in Bronx, New York. The ministry currently has two satellite locations in Ghana (Fetteh Kakraba branch in Accra and Bussie branch in Wa) and two more branches in Kenya (Kisii and Nyamira).

Born into the family of His Lordship Justice Joseph Kow Essiem, an Appeals Court Judge in Ghana, Rev. Prince spent several years pursuing a music career in Ghana, West Africa. He was twice awarded the brightest D.J. of the Western Region in Ghana by the Western Region Spinners Association ("Westsper"). He recorded his first album in 1998, and subsequently left Ghana for the USA in 2002 on the promise of a record deal, only to be cheated and left penniless on the streets of the Bronx, NY. His dream shattered and family forsaken, he learned to be poor and hungry by coming to America!

Through a series of miraculous events, Reverend Prince landed on the doorstep of the Apostles Continuation Church, where he started out as a custodian while working another job in a factory. He received his training and ordination as an Apostolic Pastor under Head Pastor Rev. Samuel Safo Kantanka. He later became Head Pastor of Divine Power Ministry.

The congregation continues to grow globally as The Word is ministered to families from a variety of backgrounds, geographic locations, and ethnicities. Rev. Prince is now mentoring several pastors from all parts of the world to the Glory of God and the seeking first of His kingdom.

This compilation of deeper insights – "Words of Water" – is Volume I of what is likely to be a long series of the sermon-summaries that Rev. Prince has preached at various times. Many of the broadcasts are still available for viewing on Facebook (www.fb.me/DPMBronx) through the Divine Power Ministry website (DivinePowerMinistry.org).

Rev. Prince Kojo Essiem is praying that everyone who picks up a volume or watches a broadcast will be refreshed and enriched by the Love of God and the Divine Power of The Living Word.

It is recommended that the reader open Words of Water each day as a devotional reading. Its 31 chapters feed the soul for one month. Highlight the ones that are especially impactful and reread as God leads for further prayer and meditation.

"He who believes in Me [who adheres to, trusts in, and relies on Me], as the Scripture has said, 'From his innermost being will flow continually rivers of living water.'" —John 7:38

## *Do not see the size of your enemy, but know how great and powerful is your God*

Main texts: Exodus 3:14; John 14:6

Are you facing large, maybe even huge problems in your life?  Does it seem like you are powerless to do anything?  Are you afraid to get out of bed?    Then you are probably focused on the wrong thing!

This week's message encourages you to focus on how great and powerful God is and how, in comparison, the enemies you see (your problems) are ready to be conquered!  First, turn your focus on to the greatness and power of God.  Know that the Creator of **EVERYTHING** is fully capable of handling **ANYTHING** you may be facing. God has been overcoming the enemies of His faithful people since recorded time.

Let's look at the example of Moses. In Chapter 2 of the book of Exodus, we get the back story of Moses. He grew up in the house of the Egyptian Pharaoh, the most powerful ruler on Earth at that time, through a series of miraculous events. He was; however, an Israelite and they were an entire nation under the bondage of slavery for more than 400 years. Moses tried to take matters into his own hands (without God) and murdered one of the Egyptian Task Masters (v12). When he tried to intercede among some quarrelling Israelites, they called him out for the murder, and he fled as a fugitive. He took on a new identity as a sheep herder and laid low for 40 years!  But his story does not end there…

God had a plan for Moses, just like he has a plan for each of us. God called Moses (Exodus 3) to do something that seemed **IMPOSSIBLE!** God told Moses that he had to go back and face a new Pharaoh and tell him that he must free the nearly 2 Million Israelites under slavery – the entire economic foundation of Egypt. Now stop and think about this as it relates to you.

Have things from your past made it seem like you can never amount to much?  Are you running away from something you are ashamed of?  Have you been "stuck" doing something for a long time that you know is not what you were intended to be doing? Do you see the changes you are considering as having significant financial hurdles? Is what you are facing seemingly impossible, then you can relate to Moses!

Like any human facing seemingly impossible odds, Moses asks God (Ex 3:11) "Who am I that I should go to Pharaoh and bring the Israelites out of Egypt?"  But that was the wrong question because Moses was focused on the power and size of the enemy and not the greatness and power of the One he was asking. In effect, Moses was saying, "there's no way I can do this!" And he was right.

Notice how God answers Moses. God does not get angry with Moses for asking. God simply reassures Moses that He will be with Moses (v 12) and then, as Moses is still having reservations as to how all this will happen, God reminds Moses, "I AM and WHAT I AM, and WHAT I WILL BE WHAT I AM; and He said, You shall say this to the Israelites, I AM has sent me to you." (v 14). God is telling Moses that it is not about Moses. God is telling Moses that 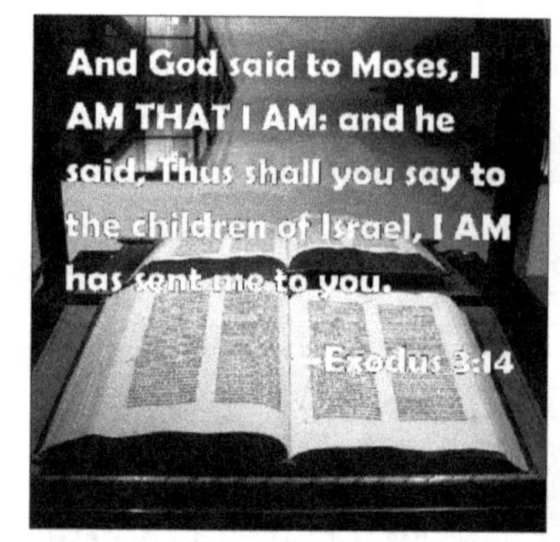



there is NOTHING that God cannot handle. By saying that "I AM" is sending Moses, God is really telling Moses that God [Father /Son/Spirit] is unique among anything. He alone exists apart and beyond everything. He alone is all-powerful, all-knowing, everywhere at once, and beyond human names!  And this fact that God reveals to Moses is all Moses needs to know to overcome the enemies /obstacles /problems he, as a limited human, sees before him. And, of course we see that God does deliver the Israelites out of slavery with Moses as their leader. God was truthful!

But how, you ask, does the story of Moses relate to me?  How does this event that happened nearly 3,500 years ago have anything to do with what I am facing today? How can I overcome all these big problems facing me in my life? Does God have a plan for me? These are exactly the questions Jesus' disciples had in their minds as context to our second text, John 14:6.

The disciples had just finished the Last Supper with Jesus. He has told them He was going to leave them and prepare a place for them in Heaven (John 14:3). They were in a panic because they only saw a path of worldly obstacles and enemies. They too, just like Moses, were not focused on the power and greatness of God standing before them.

As they pressed him further, He answered, "I am the Way the Truth and the Life; no one comes to the Father except by (through) me." Sound familiar? The same God telling Moses that He is all Moses needed is the same God telling His disciples the very same thing 1,500 years later!

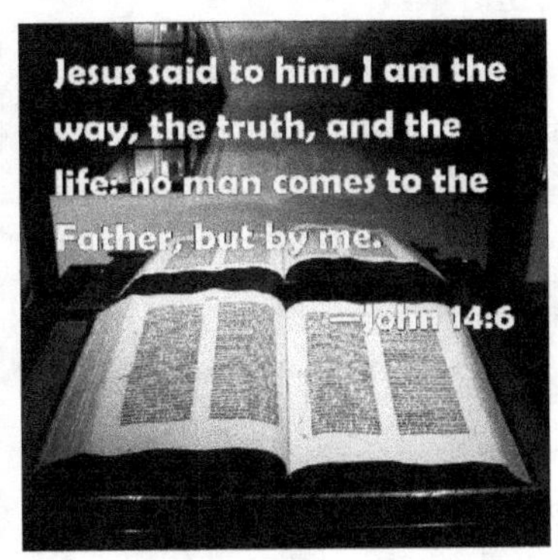


And He is there, right now, if you have made Him your Savior and Lord, telling you through the Holy Spirit, FOCUS ON ME – I AM WHO I AM – I AM ALL YOU NEED! Jesus wants you to open your eyes and see the truth. Later in that same chapter of John, Jesus explains how it will work and says, (John 14:15-16) " 15 "If you [really] love Me, you will keep and obey My commandments. 16 And I will ask the Father, and He will give you another [c]Helper (Comforter, Advocate, Intercessor—Counselor, Strengthener, Standby), to be with you forever—17 the Spirit of Truth, whom the world cannot receive [and take to its heart] because it does not see Him or know Him, but you know Him because He (the Holy Spirit) remains with you continually and will be in you."

We know this same truth applies to all who have accepted the Gospel of Jesus Christ by faith! Hebrews 13:8 confirms that Jesus Christ is [eternally changeless, always] the same yesterday and today and forever.

So, dearly beloved, do not focus on the size of your problems, your enemies, your past failures, or your present challenges, but know how great and powerful is your God! He is here for you and will supply your every need to fulfill His plan for your life as a disciple of Jesus Christ.

*May the Peace of Christ be with you always!*

# WORDS OF WATER No. 2

"He who believes in Me [who adheres to, trusts in, and relies on Me], as the Scripture has said, 'From his innermost being will flow continually rivers of living water.'" —John 7:38

(For Further Study)

## *Do not see the size of your enemy, but know how great and powerful is your God*

Main Texts: John 11:40; John 14:6

Many people are hurting significantly as a result of the pandemic. Perhaps you have missed out on an important event, seen the loss of your income, or even had to face the death of someone close to you? Are you so busy trying to "make things right" among the chaos that you are facing obstacles you have no idea how to deal with?

In today's message we hear about Lazarus coming out of the grave after being buried four days earlier. How could this have been possible? Let's go a bit deeper and look at how great and powerful is your God!

In the Gospel account of Dr. Luke, chapter 10:38-42, we are introduced to two sisters, Martha and Mary. Mary sits at the feet of Jesus during His visit, while Martha stays caught up in busy work. Their brother was Lazarus. By John 10; however, the situation is very different. Lazarus had been sick for several days and the sisters had sent word to Jesus. By the time Jesus decided to arrive, Lazarus had died and been buried for four days. To Martha and Mary, the situation seemed completely hopeless. Their entire lives were upside down. There was no way for them to be supported, there was nothing but grief and sadness all around them. They could only see the size of their problems as Jesus comes on the scene.

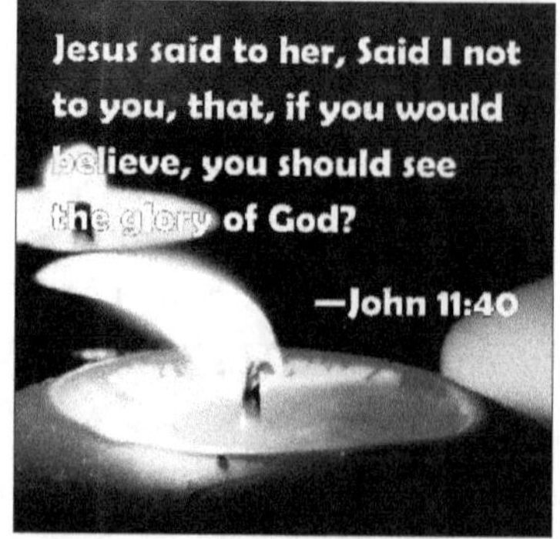

Are you feeling like Marth and Mary? Have you called upon the Lord but have yet to see His answer?  Has your situation gotten worse instead of better? Or maybe you have just stopped thinking about how great and powerful is your God? And this is the lesson of Martha and Mary that gives us all hope and joy – the good news of Jesus Chris!

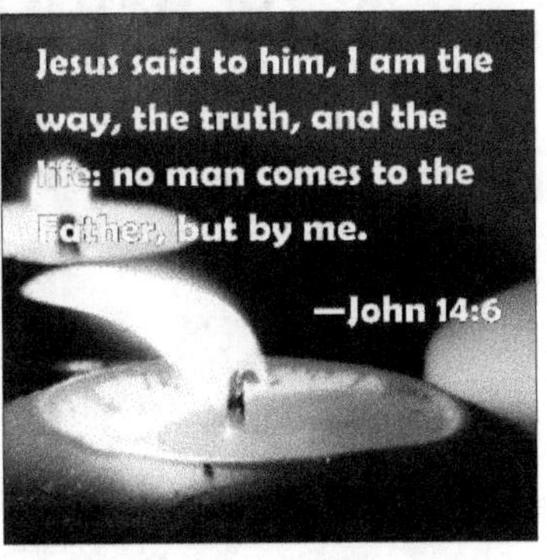


As Jesus approaches the grave, He engages Martha and then Mary with several questions about their faith. He even asks Martha directly, "Do you believe this" (John 11:26). He sees their faith and their sorrow and Jesus weeps with them in compassion. But then He commands the stone be removed and Martha gives protest about how bad it will smell. So Jesus tells her these words, the same words He tells all of His believers: 40 Jesus said to her, "Did I not say to you that if you believe [in Me], you will see the glory of God [the expression of His excellence]?"(Amplified)   He then commands Lazarus to come out of the grave and Lazarus comes walking out alive again!

Whatever you are facing in this life, the answer is always the same – Jesus!  Do not let the size of your enemies, or the size of your problems and challenges lie to you or steal away your life. Jesus says to us the same thing He told His disciples before He went to the cross (John 14:6) 6 … "I   am   the [only] Way [to   God] and   the [real] Truth   and the [real] Life; no one comes to the Father but through Me." (Amplified)

We do not know God's timing in answering our prayers. But we can stand upon the eternal, life-giving greatness and power of Jesus Christ when facing anything!

*May the Peace of Christ be with you always!*

# WORDS OF WATER No. 3

"He who believes in Me [who adheres to, trusts in, and relies on Me], as the Scripture has said, 'From his innermost being will flow continually rivers of living water.'" —John 7:38

(For Further Study)

### *Do not see the size of your enemy, but know how great and powerful is your God*

Main Texts: 1 Samuel 17:11 and 47; John 14:6

Do you know people who are stuck? Do you have friends that are endlessly telling you about how big their problems are? Maybe you are associated with a business, a sports team, or even a social or ministry group that just cannot seem to move forward? Well it just might be time for you to step up and help them all see that the enemies they face are not bigger than the God you serve!

In today's broadcast we talked about David facing Goliath. If you have never read the full account, it can be found in the book of 1 Samuel, chapter 17. The entire Army of the nation of Israel was standing still on the battlefield. King Saul of Israel, along with three of David's brothers were part of this great Army. They were lined up for battle against the Philistines, but the Philistine champion, Goliath, had come out to challenge anyone in the Israeli Army to a "winner takes all" contest. This means that if the person representing Israel lost, the entire nation of Israel would become slaves to the Philistines. The stakes could not get any higher!

Goliath steps forward and poses the challenge to Saul and his Army. Now keep in mind that Saul was the anointed King of Israel. Back in 1 Samuel 9-12 we read how God had directed Samuel to anoint Saul after some miraculous signs. But by this point in time, Saul and the rest of his Army had lost their focus on God and



7

could only see the size of their enemy standing before them. It says in chapter 17, v 11, how they all reacted to Goliath's challenge. [11] When Saul and all Israel heard these words of the Philistine, they were dismayed and greatly afraid. Nobody in their ranks was willing to step forward to take on Goliath. King Saul went as far as promising zero taxes (for his extended family) for life AND the hand of his daughter in marriage (meaning an instant appointment to leadership in the country) to anyone who would go and defeat the enemy. But everyone remained frozen in fear!

David was not even in the Army of Israel. He was too young. He was there to deliver some food to his three older brothers and to bring back word on how they were doing to his aging father. He comes upon the scene and cannot believe what he is hearing and seeing. David cannot understand why everyone is standing around letting this enemy trash

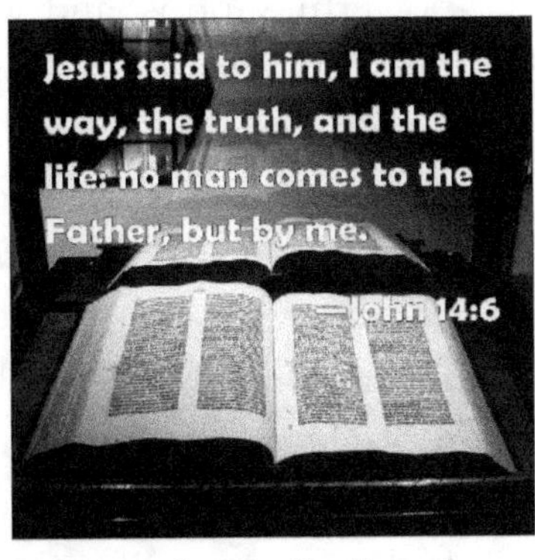


talk about them and their God!  David goes forward to talk directly to King Saul about the situation. At first the King dismisses David as being too young and inexperienced. But David gives his testimony about how God had enabled him to protect his sheep by defeating bears and lions.

There is a key lesson here that should not be missed. David knew his God. David had experienced God's deliverance and provision. We all need to remember that God is always preparing us for the battles ahead. God is building our testimony up to give us confidence and to be an inspiration for others. If you are facing something challenging, if you are part of a group that cannot seem to move forward against obstacles, look not at those obstacles but on the greatness and power of your God! Reflect upon what God has already done in your life. He loved you so much that He died for you on a cross to pay the price for your sins. He gives you His Holy Spirit to dwell within you when you repent of your sins and accept His saving grace through faith. He continues to guide you and strengthen you through the trials of life. And He has told you the way to hold on to truth and life eternal:  "[a]I am the [only] Way [to

God] and the [real] Truth and the [real] Life; no one comes to the Father but through Me. (John 14:6 Amp). So, no matter what you, or a group you are a part of is facing, know that your God is all you need. Turn the battles over to God and let Him guide you to victory!

David did not need the armor of Saul the King, even through the King tried to force David to wear it. David knew that the battle was not about him! David focused on his God, how great and powerful God is, and walked out to face this giant enemy. His parting words to both the entire Army of Israel and directly to Goliath in v 47: [47] "and that this entire assembly may know that the Lord does not save with the sword or with the spear; for the battle is the Lord's and He will hand you over to

us." He proceeded to slay Goliath with one smooth stone God had given him out of a riverbank that he had in his pocket. In one act of faith, after years of seeing what God was doing in his life, David defeated the biggest enemy of his country! This gave encouragement to the entire Army, and they went on to plunder the Philistines.

No matter what you are facing today. No matter what your friends or a group you belong to is facing today. Stand upon the power and greatness of God!

*May the Peace and Love of Jesus Christ be with you always!*

# WORDS OF WATER No. 4

"He who believes in Me [who adheres to, trusts in, and relies on Me], as the Scripture has said, 'From his innermost being will flow continually rivers of living water.'" —John 7:38

## *AWAKEN!*
## *SO THE NAME OF THE LORD WILL BE GLORIFIED*

Main Texts: Psalm 19:1; Isaiah 43:6-7; John 17:4-5; Ephesians 2:10

Do you feel like you just can't get out of bed some days? Are you afraid to face your reality? Maybe you just feel like there is a fog encircling you and you cannot see your pathway clearly? Today's broadcast is a message of conviction and hope for you!

We start in the book of Proverbs, chapter 6, verses 6-11. Solomon, the wealthiest man to ever walk the planet, is giving a stern warning about being lazy, or thinking that by avoiding hard work in life one can ever experience anything but the same poverty (of body, mind and spirit) as the aimless traveler, or face the helplessness of want like facing someone with a gun pointed at you. But what does Solomon point to as a template

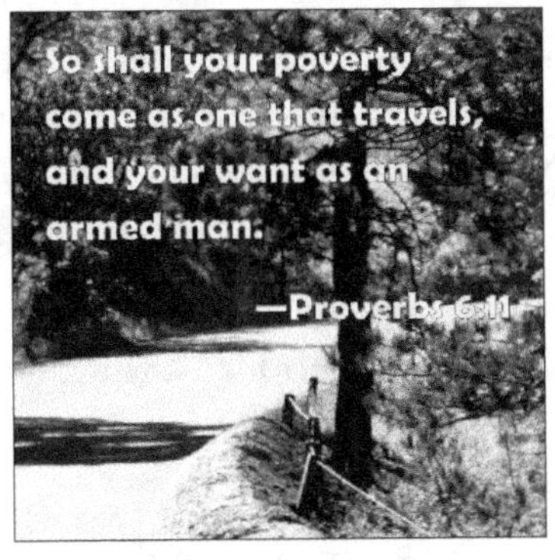



for success? Of all things in nature, he points to the lowly ants! Even the ants on the ground know to gather food in summer to prepare for winter. God has given them this instinct, and the ants do not need to be told by some authority figure like a chief or ruler. It is just who they are. It is just how they were created.

To awaken from the fog, to awaken from the sleep that is robbing us from the life we were created for, we must remember why we exist. Psalm 19:1 [Amp] says: The heavens are telling of the glory of God; And the expanse [of heaven] is declaring the work of His hands. This means that everything was created to give God glory! All of us were created to give God glory! You may have mistakenly thought that God was standing by to bless all the plans you have made to get rich and live a comfortable life the way the world has defined it. And if that is your perspective, you have been lulled asleep to the truth. God makes it crystal clear through His Prophet Isaiah: (43:6-7): "...Bring My sons from far way And My daughters from the ends of the earth, [7]Everyone who is called by My Name, ***Whom I have created for My glory***, Whom I have formed, even whom I have made." [emphasis added]. God wants us all to awaken so that the name of the Lord will be glorified!

What does it mean then to glorify the name of the Lord and how do we do that?  Everyone has a name. Typically, your name identifies you to your family. Sometimes names give insights to the day you were born, or perhaps the position you hold, or even the legacy of someone in your family tree. Have you ever heard someone say, "I was named after my great grandfather (or grandmother), who was...<someone of noteworthiness>"? And most people take some pride in their name. They aspire to bring credit to their family (name) by their accomplishments. This is admirable, but it is far less than what God has planned for us as His creation.

We learned last week about the name of God, "I AM." To understand how we are to bring glory to the name of God, we need only to turn to Jesus, the answer to every question. Jesus, as he was about to go to the cross and die to pay the price for all of our sins, talked to His Father and said, "[4]I have glorified You [down here] on the earth by [a]completing the work that You gave Me to do. [5]Now, Father, glorify Me together with Yourself, with the glory *and* majesty that I had with You before the world existed." (John 17:4-5 AMP) Jesus is God, He is part of God and calls us to be part of His family through faith. But do you see how He gave glory to God – He ***"completed the work You gave Me to do."*** It was not work that Jesus made up. It was not work that made Jesus rich or comfortable. But it was the work God gave Him to bring glory to God and Himself as God. This is the work that makes us higher than ants! Therefore, we must all AWAKEN!

Paul summarizes today's theme perfectly in the context of his letter to the believers in a city called Ephesus. In Ephesians 2:10 [AMP], the

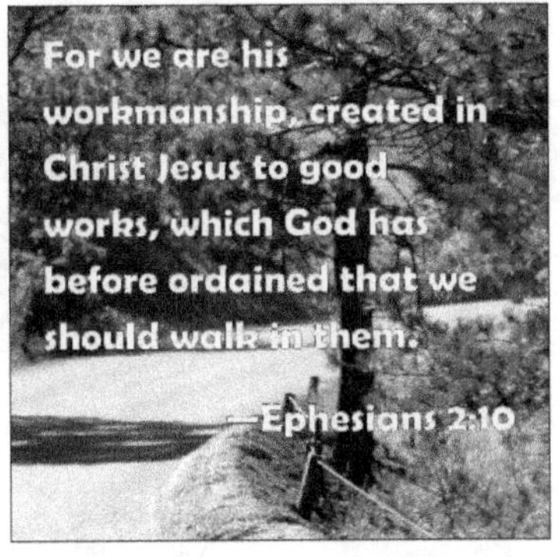


Holy Spirit tells Paul to write, "[10] For we are His workmanship [His own master work, a work of art], created in Christ Jesus [reborn from above—spiritually transformed, renewed, ready to be used] for good works, which God prepared [for us] beforehand [taking paths which He set], so that we would walk in them [living the good life which He prearranged and made ready for us]." You see, we are not created to fall asleep and be lost in this world's sinfulness. Nothing you are facing can stand in the way of why you were created. If you have accepted Jesus Christ as your Lord and Savior, you have a new name = Christian, and you have work that He has given you. Awaken, so the name of The Lord will be glorified!

*May the peace and love of Christ be with you always!*

# WORDS OF WATER No. 5

"He who believes in Me [who adheres to, trusts in, and relies on Me], as the Scripture has said, 'From his innermost being will flow continually rivers of living water.'" —John 7:38

(For Further Study)
### *AWAKEN!*
### *SO THE NAME OF THE LORD WILL BE GLORIFIED*

Main Texts: Proverbs 6:6-11; Matthew 17:21

Tired of facing financial worries?  Are you thinking that "forces of evil" are too much for you to overcome?  Maybe you just want to crawl under the blankets and go to sleep? Today's broadcast has a message for you!  Let's go deeper and discover what God's Word tells us.

We start in the book of Proverbs, chapter 6, verses 6-11. The guidance from God is to do the opposite of what our human reactions tell us we should do. Instead of giving up or crawling under those blankets, we need to look at some examples from nature (because we often forget we are also part of God's creation!) We probably never considered ants as role models, but that is exactly where we can get some of the insights we need. Ants do not need "motivational speeches" from "charismatic leaders."  The ants instinctively know that they need to gather food in the summer to get ready for the winter. The ants do not ponder their alternatives. The ants do not crawl into their cozy ant hills and wait for things to blow over. The ants know how to go find their food and they know to store up in summer. God made them that way.

Obviously, God made humans differently than the ants. But we need to realize that He is our Creator and Provider. He gives us what we need and has provided us with instructions on how

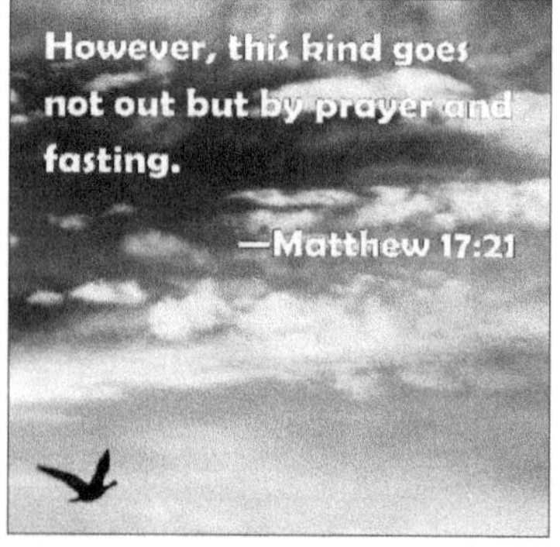

to face our problems and challenges. Once again, always look to Jesus for the answer. If you are thinking that something evil (witch, disease, curse, whatever) is prohibiting you from what God has called you to do, then follow the guidance that Jesus gave in Matthew 17:20-21 [Amp], "[20] He answered, "Because of your little faith [your lack of trust and confidence in the power of God]; for I assure you *and* most solemnly say to you, [a]if you have [living] faith the size of a mustard seed, you will say to this mountain, 'Move from here to there,' and [if it is God's will] it will move; and nothing will be impossible for you. [21] [b][But this kind of demon does not go out except by prayer and fasting.]" In other words, AWAKEN, so the name of The Lord will be glorified!

Have you ever seen a mustard seed? Here is a picture (courtesy of susannorris.org)

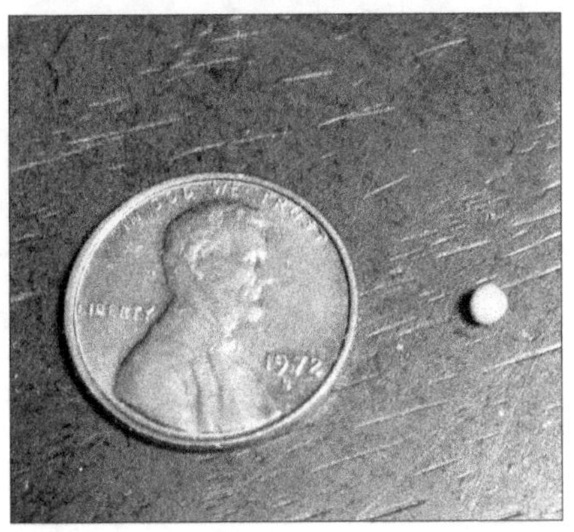

Isn't it ironic that this picture shows a mustard seed in relationship to money? You might think your problems are based upon your bank account, but God only cares about the size of your faith! If you want to show yourself what a deeper faith might look like, Jesus says to fast and pray. Go without food for just one meal. And while you do that, meditate and talk with God about how He has provided you with all your previous meals throughout your life until now. See if things do not start to look differently. Talk to Him about what you are facing while you take a proper "time out" by fasting.

God does not tell us to crawl under the blankets. God tells us to fast and pray, to EXERCISE our faith. When we fast and pray, we are, in one sense, storing up for the winter – we store up the memories of how God has been faithful to His Words so that when we face other challenges, we know He is always with us. And we are assured by the words of Jesus, "NOTHING IS IMPOSSIBLE." How wonderful is God that He requires so little of us and gives so much of Himself! He loved us so much, in fact, that He came down from Heaven and paid our debts (for sin) in full! He has completely overcome any power that anything evil could lay claim to about us. Any mountains of problems, "evil forces," or whatever your mountains are composed of, can all be moved out of your way with a small (small as a mustard seed) act of faith. Maybe, just maybe, that mustard seed-act is simply getting out from under those blankets and taking the advice of the ants — AWAKEN, so the name of the Lord will be glorified!

*May the peace and love of Christ be with you always!*

# WORDS OF WATER No. 6

"He who believes in Me [who adheres to, trusts in, and relies on Me], as the Scripture has said, 'From his innermost being will flow continually rivers of living water.'" —John 7:38

## *Let your decisions bring hope and blessings to those around you*

Main Texts: John 3:16; Genesis 13:10-16; Matthew 5:16; Acts 5:1-10

The last few weeks have touched upon some key topics related to changing your perspectives. Two weeks ago, we talked through changing your point of view from the size of your enemy or problems to focusing on the greatness and power of God. Last week was all about waking up from the sleep and laziness imposed on you by the worldly challenges – and looking to the ants as the example of taking care in due season because God has a purpose for your life. But is the main point to do the above to just help yourself? Do we call upon God simply to make us rich and comfortable? Do we busy ourselves just to store up treasure for retirement?  Are you betting your life on that?

The central message of the Gospel is giving from abundant love. In John 3:16 (AMP), Jesus explained it clearly, "[16] For God so greatly loved *and* dearly prized the world that He [even] gave up His only begotten ([a]unique) Son, so that whoever believes in (trusts in, clings to, relies on) Him shall not perish (come to destruction, be lost) but have eternal (everlasting) life. God could have let us all go to hell under the burden of a sin debt none of us can pay. But instead, He made an incredible decision that now brings hope and blessings to everyone who believes. Jesus chose to be the One who would come down out of Heaven to give glory to God and bless everyone by paying their sin debt in full (Revelation 1). This is grace, or unmerited favor, and it is what God expects of everyone who has accepted His grace (salvation) by faith.

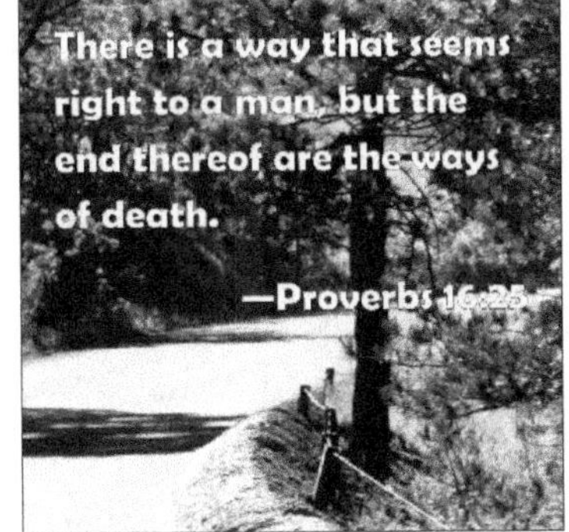

God created all of us in His image (Gen 1:26), which means He fully intended us to imitate His Spirit of giving out of love. But mankind rebelled and brought sin into our world. Since the fall, God has been giving us example after example of how we are to behave and why. Once we accept His free gift of salvation by grace through faith, the Holy Spirit can work through us to share the Gospel and bless others with our material blessings. This too, gives glory to God! In other words, we become gracious, we become more like Jesus. Today we look at the Old Testament story of Lot and Abram and the New Testament teachings of Jesus along with a story from the book of Acts. We will see how we are to let our decisions bring hope and blessings to those around us!

By Chapter 13 in Genesis, Abram (who would later become Abraham) had answered God's call and God's promise of a great blessing and left his father's homeland with all his wife and his nephew, Lot, since he was already 75 years old and had no children to help him. He had no idea where he was going, he was just taking God at His word. The two men

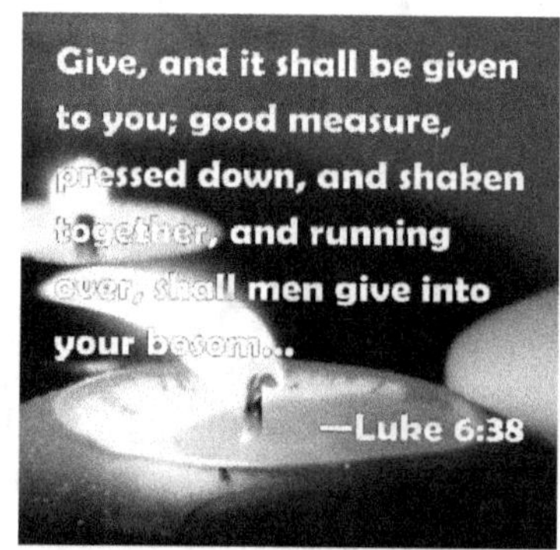


had many herds of animals that were getting mixed up to the point where their hired hands were starting to argue. So, Abram gave Lot the opportunity to pick whatever portion of the land he wanted. Abram would take what was left. Lot did not consult with God. Lot did not consider anything except himself as we are told in Genesis 13:10-11 (AMP), [10] And Lot looked and saw that everywhere the Jordan Valley was well watered. Before the Lord destroyed Sodom and Gomorrah, [it was all] like the garden of the Lord, like the land of Egypt, as you go to Zoar. [11] Then Lot chose for himself all the Jordan Valley and [he] traveled east. So they separated. Lot did not make his decision to bring hope to Abram or to bless him. Lot was not gracious. Lot went East and ended up in Sodom (yes, as in Sodom and Gomorrah), but Abram then went West and God showed him the 'promised land." This story shows us that the most beneficial choice for "worldly" gain may not be a blessing if we exclude God from our decision process. By Genesis chapter 19, we see Lot's "lot in life" with the destruction of Sodom and Gomorrah and the incestuous offspring that become the enemies of the Israelites down through the ages. Short term gains can lead to long-term misery.

In the New Testament, Jesus teaches all of us to make decisions and use our work to be a blessing to others and give glory to God. In Matthew 5:16 (AMP) we read Jesus' words," [16] Let your light so shine before men that they may see your [a]moral excellence *and* your praiseworthy, noble, *and* good deeds *and* [b]recognize *and* honor *and* praise *and* glorify your Father Who is in heaven. In the early days of the Church, many who had worldly wealth contributed to the common needs of the fellowship of believers to give them hope and blessings as God put on their hearts. This was even beyond the tithe!

But some did not make their decisions wisely – to give hope to others and bless those around them. We are given the account of a husband and wife who sold a piece of land and then decided to lie about it to Peter. In Acts 5: 2-5 Ananias, the husband, comes in and tells his lie about his donation. [2] And with his wife's knowledge *and* connivance he kept back *and* wrongfully appropriated some of the proceeds, bringing only a part and putting it at the feet of the apostles. [3] But Peter said, Ananias, why has Satan filled your heart that you should lie to *and* attempt to deceive the Holy Spirit, and should [in violation of your promise] withdraw secretly *and* appropriate to your own use part of the price from the sale of the land? [4] As long as it remained unsold, was it not still your own? And [even] after it was sold, was not [the money] at your disposal *and* under your control? Why then, is it that you have proposed *and* purposed in your heart to do this thing? [How could you have the heart to do such a deed?] You have not [simply] lied to men [playing false and showing yourself utterly deceitful] but to God. [5]

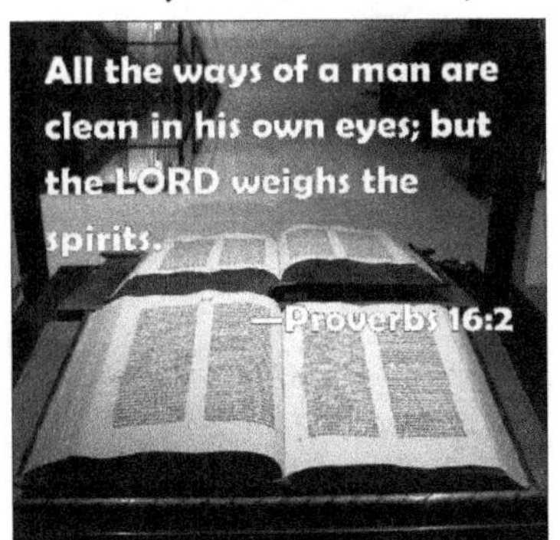


Upon hearing these words, Ananias fell down and died. And great dread *and* terror took possession of all who heard of it. And right after that (verses 6-10), Sapphira, his wife did the same thing with the same outcome!

God looks at our hearts. We are to emulate Jesus and make our decisions to give others hope and bless those around us. Make sure you are in prayer over how God can use you, and how He has blessed you, to shine light into this dark world!

*May the peace and love of Christ be with you always!*

"He who believes in Me [who adheres to, trusts in, and relies on Me], as the Scripture has said, 'From his innermost being will flow continually rivers of living water.'" —John 7:38

(For Further Study)

## *Let your decisions bring hope and blessings to those around you*

Main Texts: Matthew 25:29;35-36;40 Proverbs 19:17 Isaiah 58:7

Ever wonder why you may be blessed with good income, position, or power in this life? Have you decided that, "what's mine is mine for my enjoyment"? Today's broadcast encourages all of us to make our decisions from the eternal perspective. Let's dive deeper into what God is telling all of us.

In the last days of Jesus's earthly ministry, His followers were asking Him about how the end of time would look like (Matthew 24). Jesus told them that nobody knows the exact time, but to stay ready by following what He had taught them. Then He went on to tell them several parables, which are stories designed to help us understand what we

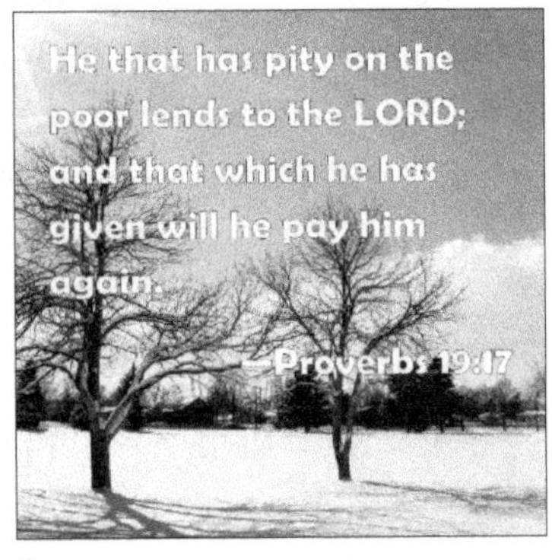


have not yet experienced, or do not understand, through situations that are familiar to us.

In Matthew, Chapter 25, Jesus tells of the ten virgins waiting on the groom (verses 1-13); the wealthy property owner who entrusts "talents" to three different subordinates and who each one of them decided what to do with what they had been given (verses 14-30). It is in this parable that last week's broadcast about laziness is also reinforced. The subordinate who managed their talents best, for the highest return, were given even more from the one who was scared and lazy, (Matt 25:29 AMP) "[29] For to everyone who has will more be given, and he will be [a]furnished richly so that he will have an abundance; but from the one who does not have, even what he does have will be taken away." All our decisions have consequences!

Matthew, Chapter 25, then ends with the combination of a parable and the explanation of how it will be at the end of either all time or our personal time in this life. Jesus said we will all be separated like a shepherd separates sheep from goats. The point here is that both groups may say they are following the same shepherd, but in the end, there will be a separation and distinctions made by God. The true

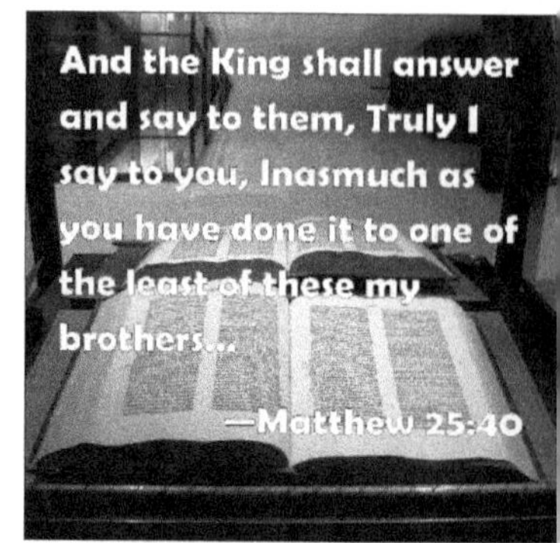


believers, who have accepted salvation by faith and then demonstrated that faith through their transformed lives (how they decided to act differently by bringing hope and blessings to those around them) will receive "…the kingdom prepared for you from the foundation of the world." (Matthew 25:34b). What decisions did those who are receiving a kingdom make? Jesus spells them out clearly in Matthew 25:35-36 AMP): "35 For I was hungry and you gave Me food, I was thirsty and you gave Me something to drink, I was a stranger and you [a]brought Me together with yourselves *and* welcomed *and* entertained *and* [b]lodged Me, 36 I was naked and you clothed Me, I was sick and you visited Me [c]with help *and* ministering care, I was in prison and you came to see Me."

Of course, if we saw Jesus in front of us and asking for something to eat we would gladly invite Him into our home and feed Him a special meal. But what is Jesus telling those He was talking to through this parable? We find out very clearly just a few verses later in Matthew 25:40 AMP, "40 And the King will reply to them, Truly I tell you, in so far as you did it for one of the least [[a]in the estimation of men] of these My brethren, you did it for Me. " We have the opportunity to make decisions that bring hope and blessings to those around us every day! These decisions have ETERNAL RAMIFICATIONS.

Nearly 500 years before Jesus came down from Heaven to pay our sin debt in full, The Holy Spirit inspired the Prophet Isaiah to warn the entire people of God, who had decided to turn away from the Lord. They forgot that the underlying purpose of prayer and fasting was to humble ourselves before God so that the bonds of wickedness will be loosened and the blessings He gives us can be shared with those in need.

Decide today that you will use what talents you have to give hope and blessings to all around you. Let the Lord Jesus use us to bless His creation through the blessings He bestows upon us. He is faithful to His word and His promises. Let us all humble ourselves with prayer and fasting that we may decide to give hope and blessings to all around us.

*May the peace and love of Christ be with you always!*

Is it not to deal your bread to the hungry, and that you bring the poor that are cast out to your house? when you see the naked...

—Isaiah 58:7

# WORDS OF WATER No. 8

"He who believes in Me [who adheres to, trusts in, and relies on Me], as the Scripture has said, 'From his innermost being will flow continually rivers of living water.'" —John 7:38

## *You will sing with joy when you put your hope in God*

Main Texts: Exodus 14:30; 15:1-2, Romans 8:28, Psalm 33:3

We are praising God that this broadcast could originate from our Church! It was so wonderful to experience fellowship and community, if still by social distancing and wearing our masks. These are such small sacrifices that we gladly make so that everyone can be safe and avoid the virus. Remember, our example is always Jesus, and He sacrificed His life so that we all can have life everlasting! It does not matter where we broadcast – we know our God is at work!

So, today's broadcast message is a message that builds upon the past few weeks. For some of us, the journey during the pandemic has been extremely difficult. We have either been ill or know someone who has been ill. Perhaps we are still mourning the loss of a close friend or loved one, the loss of a job, or even the postponing of a special event as a result of

the pandemic? Perhaps we feel like we have been running from this virus and we are not sure when we will ever "return to normal"?

God gives us a great example to look toward in times like we are facing today. The Nation of Israel had spent 400 years in Egypt, and most of that time under slavery by the Egyptians. But God is faithful to His promises, and He had promised them a land of their own through Abraham, whom we looked at last week. Today we look at how God delivered on His promise in Exodus chapter 14, and their reaction.

Remember the whole story?  When God led Moses to lead His people to freedom, God brought 10 significant plagues against Egypt to show the Pharaoh, and all the people from the most powerful country on the planet at that time, that God is the great "I AM," the Creator and all-powerful God.

We pick up the account in the end of Chapter 14 of Exodus, when the whole group Israelites are fleeing Egypt and they hear that the Army of Egypt is now chasing them. They come up against the Red Sea and it looks like they will all get slaughtered. But what does God do?  Even in the wake of the critics who were yelling at Moses for leading them to certain slaughter, God tells Moses to lift up his arms and get helpers to keep his arms raised, and the sea separates and they cross on dry land (Exodus 14:13-29 AMP). And in v.30 we read: "[30] Thus the Lord saved Israel that day from the hand of the Egyptians, and Israel saw the Egyptians dead upon the seashore."  God had been working all the while to bring deliverance and fulfill His promises, but the Israelites just could not see any hope in their situation. In the overwhelming aftermath of this miracle of miracles, their reaction was a new song of joy!

Exodus Chapter 15:1-21 is a beautiful song of praise and worship to God almighty. In fact, as Moses gets done leading everyone in this song, his sister, Miriam leads all the women in continuing to sing and dance as they do, "[20] Then Miriam the prophetess, the sister of Aaron, took a timbrel in her hand, and all the women went out after her with

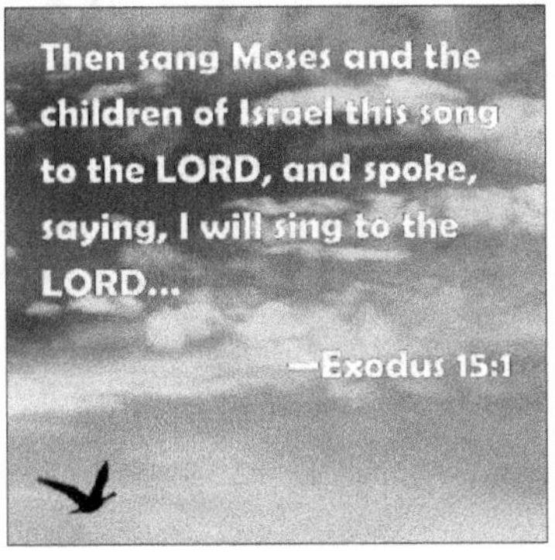


timbrels and dancing. [21] And Miriam responded to them, Sing to the Lord, for He has triumphed gloriously and is highly exalted; the horse and his rider He has thrown into the sea." (Ex 15:20-21 AMP) Their enemy vanquished, the Nation of Israel had put their hope in the Lord and were singing a new song!

The Israelites could not see God at work on their behalf before, when all they saw was slavery and then the plagues in Egypt. They did not know that God was working behind the scenes to bring good out of what looked like hopelessness. Sometimes it is difficult for us as well, even though we have the advantage of the Bible, with all these wonderful accounts. But we can walk on dry ground through the seas of problems all around us by remembering, (Romans 8:28 AMP),

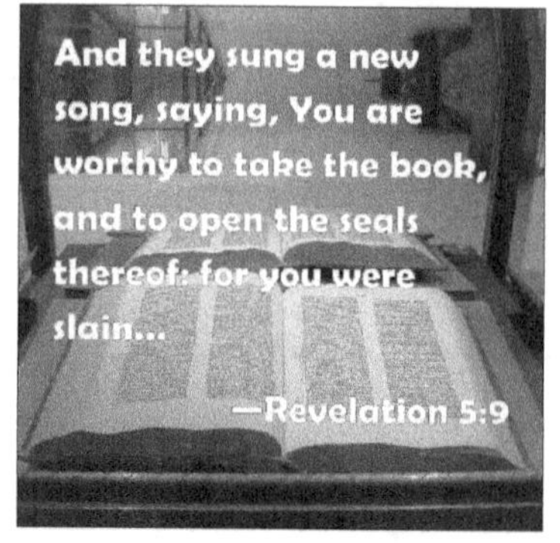


"[28] We are assured and know that [[a]God being a partner in their labor] all things work together and are [fitting into a plan] for good to and for those who love God and are called according to [His] design and purpose." We just need to place our faith and our hope in God and we will be singing a new song of joy!

Whenever we stop and reflect on what God has done, and is doing in our lives, we have no better outlet for our joy than to sing. Think about where we would be if Jesus had not paid the price for our sins and made everlasting life in Heaven assured. We claim victory over sin because of what Jesus did for us on that cross. In fact, we are told that the Elders, the Angels, and all Creatures in Heaven rejoice and sing a new song because Jesus is worthy of all praise and glory, "[9] And [now] they sing a new song, saying, You are worthy to take the scroll and to break the seals that are on it, for You were slain (sacrificed), and with Your blood You purchased men unto God from every tribe and language and people and nation." Rev 5:9 AMP)

Put your hope in God and get ready to sing a new song of joy!

*May the peace and love of Christ be with you always!*

# WORDS OF WATER No. 9

"He who believes in Me [who adheres to, trusts in, and relies on Me], as the Scripture has said, 'From his innermost being will flow continually rivers of living water.'" —John 7:38

(For Further Study)
## *You will sing with joy when you put your hope in God*

Main Texts: 1 Samuel 16:23; Psalm 33; Psalm 117

Have you ever heard a song on the radio, and it took you to a place and time in your life that you remember vividly?  Have you ever heard one of your favorite songs and it changed your mood or disposition immediately?  Songs have a powerful effect on us because we are all created in the image of God and He loves to hear us singing to Him. We know this because King David is often described as a man after God's own heart (Acts 13:22) and David wrote many of the Psalms in the Bible.

In fact, before David slew Goliath, he was called upon to play his songs before King Saul to fend off evil spirits: 23 So it came about that whenever the [evil] spirit from God was on Saul, David took a harp and played it with his hand; so Saul would be refreshed and be well, and the evil spirit would leave him. (1Samuel 16:23 AMP) Whenever we are praising God and

giving Him all glory and honor, there is nothing that can come between the flow of His love!

But why are these Psalms (the Greek word translates to songs of praise) so powerful?  The answer is the theme for today's broadcast, "You will sing with joy when you put your hope in God."  Open the Book of Psalms and see for yourself. We will dive a bit deeper here but please spend some time reading and singing aloud some of the Psalms referenced. Let's start with the shortest Psalm and the smallest chapters in the whole Bible because it exemplifies the awesome power of these songs: (Psalm 117 AMP)

O praise the Lord, all you nations!
Praise Him, all you people!
² For His lovingkindness prevails over us [and we triumph and
overcome through Him],
And the truth of the Lord endures forever.
Praise the Lord! (Hallelujah!)

In these two short verses we see the 3 reasons why the Psalms are so powerful:

1. They tell us what we should be doing
2. They tell us why we should be doing it
3. They give us hope

What should we be doing? We should all be praising the Lord. When we are praising God, we are no longer caught up thinking about ourselves and our problems. We place ourselves in the proper order — the created beings of an almighty God!

Why should we be praising our God? Look around. God has created everything and provided all we need. His love has "prevailed over us" in that Jesus came down from Heaven and paid our sin debt in full. Jesus has prevailed over the power of sin in our lives that we may believe in Him and have eternal life connected with God. We too, can overcome this world through faith in Jesus. Jesus told us plainly (John 8:31-32 AMP): 31 So Jesus was saying to the Jews who had believed Him, "If you abide in My word [continually obeying My teachings and living in accordance with them, then] you are truly My disciples. 32 And you will know the truth [regarding salvation], and the truth will set you free [from the penalty of sin]."

Lastly, there is confirmation for hope in God in every Psalm. Look at that last phrase of Psalm 117, "and the truth of the Lord lasts forever." We can put our hope in God's truth. Jesus said above that we can know this truth and it sets us free. And when we realize this hope is really something we can count on, we must sing with joy! We must

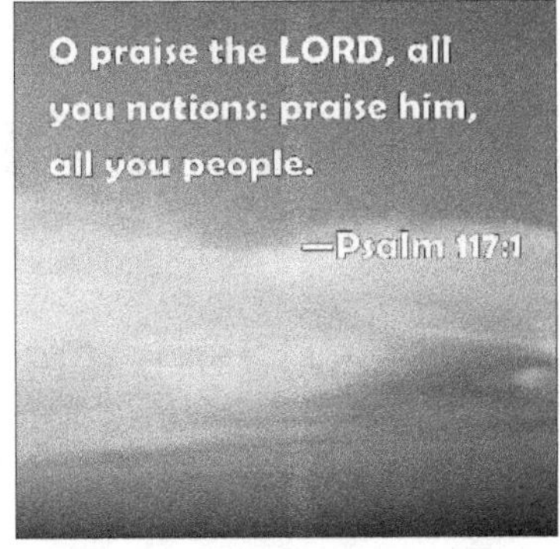


praise God! We are just wired to respond with songs of praise to express our joy.

There is a Psalm for every situation we face. God has provided us with these Psalms so that we know what we should do, why we should be doing it, and to give us hope in Him. On the following page is a list of a few of the Psalms under situational headings. Just open your Bible and allow the Holy Spirit to lead you in the song to God for the moment in life you find yourself. When you read these out loud, see if they do not change your disposition instantly and your being wants to sing the words to God. Make up your own tune and melody and enjoy doing what God created you to do. We can all sing for joy when we put our hope in God!

*May the peace and love of Christ be with you always!*

## PSALMS OF COMFORT

Psalm 23

## PSALMS FOR DEATH & DYING

Psalm 23

## PSALMS OF DELIVERANCE

Psalm 85   Psalm 120   Psalm 126   Psalm 142

## PSALMS FOR LACK of FAITH

**PSALMS OF FORGIVENESS**



**PSALMS OF HOPE AND CONFIDENCE**



**PSALMS OF PROTECTION**



**PSALMS FOR SADNESS & SORROW**



**PSALMS FOR HELP IN TIMES OF TROUBLE**



**RESPONSORIAL PSALMS FOR WEDDINGS**



**PSALMS and AFFIRMATIONS FOR WORRY, ANXIETY AND ANGUISH**

"He who believes in Me [who adheres to, trusts in, and relies on Me], as the Scripture has said, 'From his innermost being will flow continually rivers of living water.'" —John 7:38

## *Blessed is he who confesses his sins to The Lord*

Main Texts: Psalms 32:2; Isaiah 6:1-7

Today we look at how to come before The Lord and we use the examples of the thieves on the cross with Jesus as well as the Prophet Isaiah. We all want to be blessed by God, so let's explore some more of what God tells us about how He determines who He blesses.

The first thing we must recognize is sin. Any immoral act against a divine law is sin. Another word for sin is iniquity, or any behavior **not equal** to the moral standard of God. We know from Genesis Chapter 3, that mankind did what God told them not to do – they sinned. And because of sin they were forced out of the perfect relationship with God that they

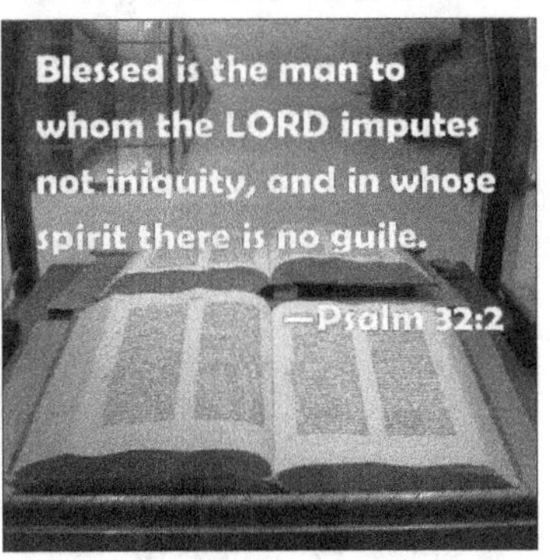


enjoyed in the garden and they were judged with a death sentence. We know that every man and woman ever since has been born with this original sin and in Romans 3:23 we see, "23 ... all have sinned and continually fall short of the glory of God." God certainly cannot bless that which is in direct opposition to His laws and directives. In fact, Romans 6:23 says, "The wages of sin is death…" and this death is eternal damnation in Hell. So, if we sin, or commit iniquities, we are doomed because God is perfectly just and because God is perfect (Psalm 18:30). Once we realize what our behaviors have really earned us in the sight of God, we are ready to understand how we must come before Him to be blessed.

Our situation of sinfulness and iniquities looks hopeless before the just and perfect standard of God. But here is the good news, 16 "For

God so [greatly] loved and dearly prized the world, that He [even] gave His [One and] [a]only begotten Son, so that whoever believes and trusts in Him [as Savior] shall not perish, but have eternal life." (John 3:16 AMP) God is also perfect in love, grace, and mercy, so He went ahead and took our judgement of death upon Himself and paid our debt in full!  But we need to understand that this first blessing of Salvation (eternal life) and any blessings we experience during our lifetime (Sanctification) are both possible **ONLY IF WE COME BEFORE THE LORD IN A TRUE SPIRIT OF CONFESSION.**

One of the best examples of the first blessing (Salvation) is the thief on the cross. There were actually two thieves, one on either side of Jesus to fulfill the scripture (Isaiah 53:12). One thief tried to use his guile, his twisted reasoning and deceit, and he said to Jesus, " [39] One of the criminals who had been hanged [on a cross beside Him] kept hurling abuse at Him, saying, "Are You not the Christ? Save Yourself and us [from death]!" (Luke 23:39 AMP) He thought that just being around Jesus was enough. He thought that he could just demand mercy and he would be blessed. His heart was hardened to his own state of sinfulness. He was not confessing his unworthiness at all.

But the other thief was different. We continue to read in Luke, " [40] But the other one rebuked him, saying, "Do you not even fear God, since you are under the same sentence of condemnation? [41] We are suffering justly, because we are getting what we deserve for what we have done; but this Man has done nothing wrong." [42] And he was saying, "Jesus, [please] remember me when You come into Your kingdom!" [43] Jesus said to him, "I assure you and most solemnly say to you, today you will be with Me in [c]Paradise."  This man was not a "church goer" during his life. He simply realized the truth of who Jesus was and

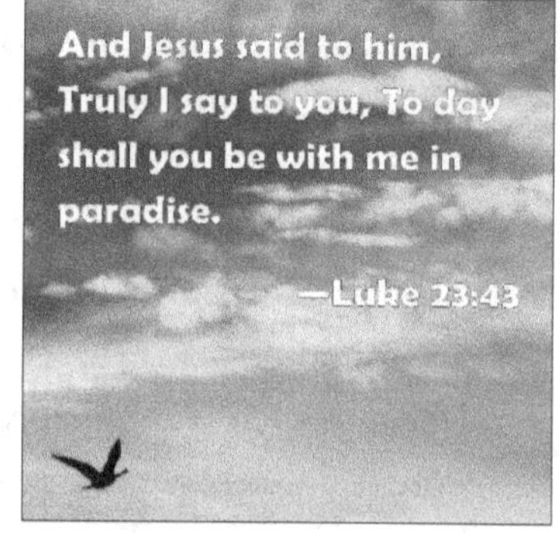


humbled himself before Jesus. He confessed his sinful state and asked for mercy. He was not holding anything back. So, Jesus gave him salvation that day and assured the thief of a place in paradise!

Both men recognized Jesus as The Christ. One was not humble or repentant and was not willing to confess his sinfulness. The other was completely humbled in the presence of Jesus, confessed his sinful state, and received the blessing of eternal life. Blessed is the man who confesses his sins to The Lord!

Does this example mean we should wait until the end of our life and try for a last-minute confession? Not at all! As soon as we realize our sinful state and believe in our hearts that Jesus paid our price in full, we should confess and be saved. "[10] For with the heart a person believes [in Christ as Savior] resulting in his justification [that is, being made righteous—being freed of the guilt of sin and made acceptable to God]; and with the mouth he acknowledges and confesses [his faith openly], resulting in and confirming [his] salvation." (Rom 10:10 AMP) We must humble ourselves and confess our sins to receive the blessing of Salvation. Even if we have been around the church our entire lives, we must be sure that we have not confessed with any guile, any reasoning that has kept a sin from God. We must "surrender all."

Let's look at a devoutly religious man, Isaiah, and this second example of great blessing that results from coming before The Lord in a true spirit of confession. We know from reading Chapters 1-5 of Isaiah that this prophet was a devout man. He gave the people of Israel many prophesies as a priest. But we have an indication that Isaiah was serving two masters – one was the King Uzziah, and the other was Almighty God. Once his ruler from this earth was dead, Isaiah was given a vision of the Most Holy God, and before this true God Isaiah makes this confession:"

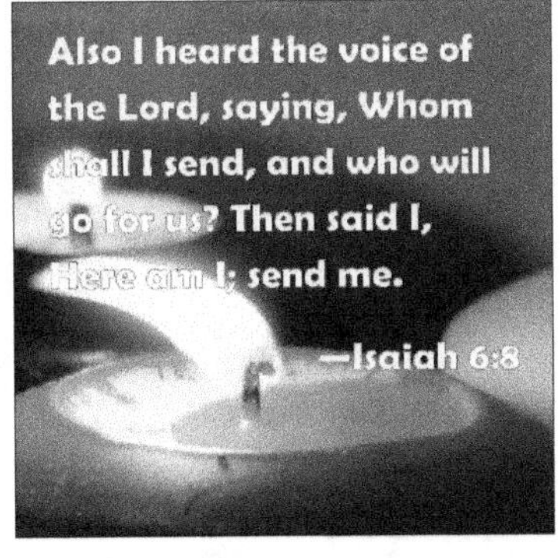


"Woe is me! For I am ruined, Because I am a man of [ceremonially] unclean lips, And I live among a people of unclean lips; For my eyes have seen the King, the Lord of hosts." (Isaiah 6:5 AMP). Because he humbled himself before God, even as a seemingly religious man, we read what God made happen next:"[7] He touched my mouth with it and said, "Listen carefully, this has touched your lips; your wickedness [your sin, your injustice, your wrongdoing] is taken away and your sin atoned for and forgiven." Through this humility and true spirit of complete confession, Isaiah ends the delay of his own blessings (his destiny).

This is the key! We must totally surrender before God. We must give up and move in the opposite direction from ALL sins. That is the meaning of repentance! For when we do, God releases His blessing and allows us to live out the life He has planned for us. Look what happened next in the life of Isaiah. The prophet was sent out to proclaim the coming of Jesus Christ into the world and God's plans for the Nation of Israel. What greater honor could any man receive? And in fact, Isaiah is known as a "Major Prophet" among all of God's prophets.

We all hold the key to the blessings. Open up your heart to God. He already knows every sin you have ever committed. You cannot hide from Him (Psalm 139:7). Simply confess your sins before God and turn away from them by the power of The Holy Spirit, and let the blessings of God's plan for your life flow. Blessed is he who confesses his sins to The Lord!

*May the peace and love of Christ be with you always!*

"He who believes in Me [who adheres to, trusts in, and relies on Me], as the Scripture has said, 'From his innermost being will flow continually rivers of living water.'" —John 7:38

(For Further Study)

## *Blessed is he who confesses his sins to The Lord*

Main Texts: Proverbs 28:13; 1 John 1:8-10; Psalm 51

The message today on confession is so vital to our Christian walk that it deserves more exploration. In this brief time together, we will dive a bit deeper into why confession always **PRECEDES** the blessings. Last time, we looked deeper into the thieves on the cross and Isaiah, so this time we will look at a few more examples. The Bible references to confessing/confession are too many to sight herein, so we will concentrate on just a few more to make this important point.

First, what do we mean when we say, "I confess my sins"? The translation of the original word (homologeó) for "confess" is a verb that means: to promise in agreement; to publicly declare or pledge. So, what we are doing is agreeing with what God already knows!

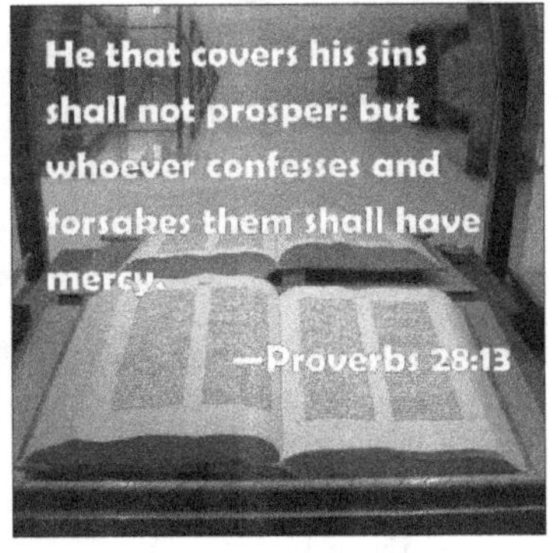


Do any of us think for one minute that we can hide anything from God? God knows our every thought (Job 21:21/Matthew 9:4). In fact, Jesus taught us that God is aware of EVERYTHING from the perspective of our motives: "<sup>15</sup>So He said to them, "You are the ones who declare yourselves just and upright in the sight of men, but God knows your hearts [your thoughts, your desires, your secrets]; for that which is highly esteemed among men is detestable in the sight of God." (Luke 16:15 AMP) This means that even when other people think we are "really good," God sees the truth about whether we are in right standing (our righteousness) to Him and His standards. So, when we confess our sins, we are simply agreeing with God on the reality of our situation.

When our pride and ego get the best of us, we all tend to think of ourselves much better than we are in the eyes of God. Then we wonder why we do not see His blessings on our lives. But blessed is he who confesses his sin to The Lord. If you doubt this truth, please turn to 1 John 1:8-10 in your Bible: "8 If we say we have no sin [refusing to admit that we are sinners], we delude ourselves and the truth is not in us. [His word does not live in our hearts.] 9 If we [freely] admit that we have sinned and confess our sins, He is faithful and just [true to His own nature and promises], and will forgive our sins and cleanse us continually from all unrighteousness [our wrongdoing, everything not in conformity with His will and purpose]. 10 If we say that we have not sinned [refusing to admit acts of sin], we make Him [out to be] a liar [by contradicting Him] and His word is not in us." <This is from the Amplified Bible to give us some additional meaning.>

So now, let's look at an example of one individual from the Old Testament, King David, and a group of people from the New Testament, the new believers at Pentecost. King David was God's anointed successor to King Saul. He was highly successful in everything he put his mind to. Then he committed adultery with his general's wife, and when she was found pregnant, David had her husband sent to the front lines so he would be killed. The entire account is written in 2 Samuel Chapters 11 and 12. But after the Prophet Nathan confronts David with his sins, David writes Psalm 51, and in it we see his confession:

3For I am conscious of my transgressions and I acknowledge them;

My sin is always before me.
4 Against You, You only, have I sinned
And done that which is evil in Your sight,
So that You are justified when You speak [Your sentence]
And faultless in Your judgment.
5 I was brought forth in [a state of] wickedness;
In sin my mother conceived me

[and from my beginning I, too, was sinful].
<sup>6</sup> Behold, You desire truth in the innermost being,
And in the hidden part [of my heart] You will make me know wisdom.
(Ps 51:3-6 AMP)

There were certainly steep consequences for David's sins. The baby died after 7 days (2 Samuel 12:18). And God put in place consequences for David's heirs. But God restored His relationship with David and allowed the second son to be the richest, most powerful man who has ever walked the planet, King Solomon. What is even more amazing, however, is that God kept His promise to David about a king in David's lineage that would have an everlasting kingdom, and that King is the King of Kings, Jesus Christ Our Lord! Blessed is he who confesses his sins to The Lord!

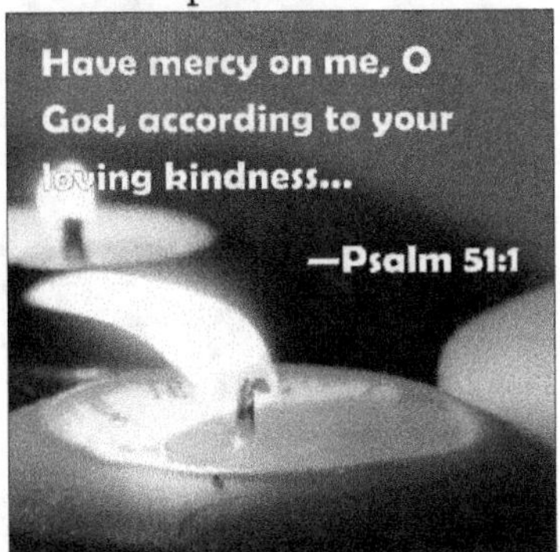


Next, let's go to an example in the New Testament. We look to another very well-known figure, Zaccheus. This man was a notorious tax collector and sinner in everyone's eyes. But he was drawn to Jesus. He climbed up in a tree just to get a look at Jesus walking by him. And when Jesus came to that place, He looked up and told Zacceus that He

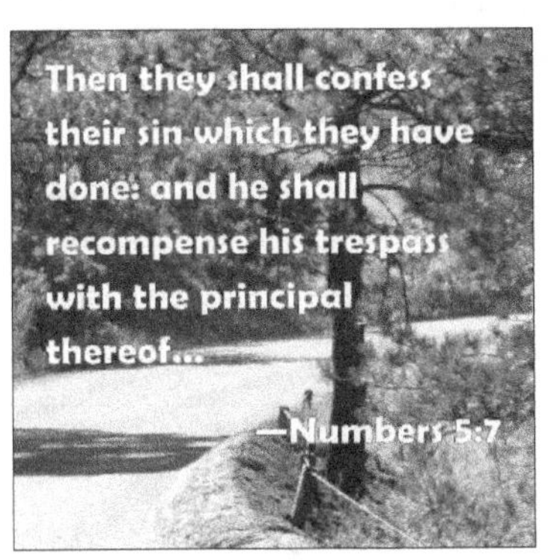


wanted to have dinner at Zaccheus' house! God saw the confession in the heart of Zaccheus. Look what happened: "<sup>6</sup> So Zaccheus hurried and came down, and welcomed Jesus with joy. <sup>7</sup> When the people saw it, they all began muttering [in discontent], "He has gone to be the guest of a man who is a [notorious] sinner." <sup>8</sup> Zaccheus stopped and said to the Lord, "See, Lord, I am [now] giving half of my possessions to the poor, and if I have cheated anyone out of anything, I will give back four times as much." [9] Jesus said to him, "Today salvation has come to this household, because he, too, is a [[b]spiritual] son of Abraham; [10] for the Son of Man has come to seek and to save that which was lost." (Luke 19:6-10 AMP) Zaccheus gave back exactly in accordance with the OT requirements found in Numbers Chapter 5. He was blessed with SALVATION! His relationship to God was on a right standing, so Jesus allowed this blessing to flow. Blessed is the man who confesses his sins to The Lord!

*May the peace and love of Christ be with you always!*

"He who believes in Me [who adheres to, trusts in, and relies on Me], as the Scripture has said, 'From his innermost being will flow continually rivers of living water.'" —John 7:38

(For Further Study)

## *Blessed is he who confesses his sins to The Lord*

Main Texts: 1 John 1:9; Matthew 6:33; John 20:29

Thus far, we have explored the confession aspects of today's broadcast. Now we can explore what it means to be "blessed." We have seen how we must recognize our sinfulness before God and agree with Him on what He already knows. We can then stand on God's promise from 1 John 1:9 (AMP): "If we [freely] admit that we have sinned and confess our sins, He is faithful and just [true to His own nature and promises], and will forgive our sins and cleanse us continually from all unrighteousness [our wrongdoing, everything not in conformity with His will and purpose]." We are cleansed from the filth of sins that prevent us from doing God's will and completing God's purpose for our lives. We are now in right standing (the state of righteousness) with God so that He may bless us. But what do these blessings look like?

When we are in right standing with God, He can release the wisdom and insights He has for us. We must all remember the foundation of our salvation: "[8] For it is by grace [God's remarkable compassion and favor drawing you to Christ] that you have been saved [actually delivered from judgment and given eternal life] through faith. And

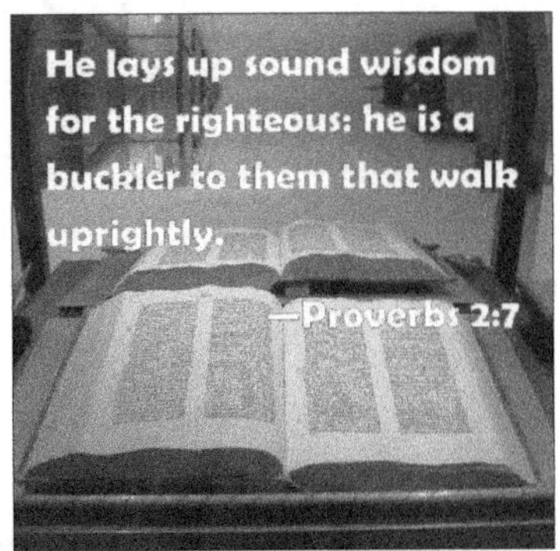


this [salvation] is not of yourselves [not through your own effort], but it is the [undeserved, gracious] gift of God; [9] not as a result of [your] works [nor your attempts to keep the Law], so that no one will [be able to] boast or take credit in any way [for his salvation]. [10] For we are His workmanship [His own master work, a work of art], created in Christ Jesus [reborn from above—spiritually transformed, renewed, ready to be used] for good works, which God prepared [for us] beforehand [taking paths which He set], so that we would walk in them [living the good life which He prearranged and made ready for us]."Ephesians 2:8-10 AMP). So, when we confess our sins and renew this right standing before God, He blesses us with wisdom to see our work within His Kingdom and the truth of His Words (Bible). He also shields us from attacks from evil.

Most of us are expecting God to bless us with material wealth, prosperity, position, honor, and respect from others. Most of us have bought into the lies on television that tell us when we live in a particular area, wear certain clothes, and dine in upscale restaurants, we "are blessed" and the world will look up to us. But that is not the way God has told us life here on Earth should work. Jesus told us all in Matthew (6:32-33 AMP): "[32] For the [pagan] Gentiles eagerly seek all these things; [but do not worry,] for your heavenly Father knows that you need them. [33] But first and most importantly seek (aim at, strive after) His kingdom and His righteousness [His way of doing and being right—the attitude and character of God], and all these things will be given to you also." God is going to provide what He determines to be our **NEEDS** to accomplish His will and His purposes for our lives. This provision is often called "God's favor."

We can look throughout the Bible to see men and women who have had God's favor upon them to accomplish the will and purposes of God in their lives: Noah (Gen 6:8), Abraham (Gen18:3), Joseph (Gen 39:21), Moses (Ex 33:17), Ruth (Ruth 2:2), Hannah (1 Sam 1:18), Samuel (1 Sam 2:26), Isaiah (Is 6:7), Nehemiah (Neh 2:18), Ester (Est 2:8), Daniel (Dan 1:9), Peter (Matt 16:17), Mary (Luke 1:30). There are many more references in Psalms, Proverbs, and in Jesus' teachings. Take some time and

familiarize yourself with these people who have found favor. We are given these many examples because God wants to demonstrate His faithfulness and give us hope!

Maybe you are thinking that these "special people" from the Bible are unique and that God's favor is not for you? Well our theme today, "Blessed is the man (and woman) who confess their sins to The Lord," applies equally to everyone who has accepted Jesus Christ as Lord and Savior! After Jesus was resurrected, He was there in physical form before His disciples. Thomas had just put his fingers on the holes in Jesus' hands and side. Then Jesus gives these wonderful words of hope to all of us: "²⁹ Jesus said to him, "Because you have seen Me, do you now believe? Blessed [happy, spiritually secure, and favored by God] are they who did not see [Me] and yet believed [in Me]." (John 20:29 AMP). Confess and be blessed!

*May the peace and love of Christ be with you always!*

# WORDS OF WATER No. 13

"He who believes in Me [who adheres to, trusts in, and relies on Me], as the Scripture has said, 'From his innermost being will flow continually rivers of living water.'" —John 7:38

## *My People Will Know My Name*

Main Texts: Isaiah 52:1-2, 6; Luke 24:49; Acts 12:4-11

Are you feeling invisible?  Do you feel like you are going through life unnoticed, unappreciated, or that you lack purpose and meaning?  Maybe you have been facing some difficulty that has you thinking you should just give up?  Today's message is for you!

It is time to WAKE UP!  God does not want His children to be lying around feeling sorry for themselves. We all need to realize that we have beautiful garments to put on. We need to realize that we, who believe in Jesus, are all part of God family and we have a new family name!

The Prophet Isaiah was given the insights and vision into what God's plan was going to be 700 years before it happened so that we can see the power and faithfulness of God to His promises. In Isaiah 52:1-2 we read:  ¹Awake, awake, put on your strength, O Zion; put on your beautiful garments, O Jerusalem, the holy city; for the uncircumcised and the unclean will no longer come into you. ² Shake yourself from the dust, arise, O captive Jerusalem; rid yourself of the chains around your neck, O captive Daughter of Zion."  He is telling Israel, and all of God's people today, that they need to wake up to the realization that God has provided "strength" and "beautiful garments."  This is strength to

face the evil of this world without fear. It is the strength of the Holy Spirit working within each of us. Our sinful selves are crucified with Christ on the cross so that the "uncircumcised and unclean" no longer have any power over us.

These beautiful garments symbolically represent our salvation through Jesus Christ. When jesus was about to leave His disciples after being resurrected, He told them: "⁴⁹ Listen carefully: I am sending the Promise of My Father [the Holy Spirit] upon you; but you are to remain in the city [of Jerusalem] until you are clothed (fully equipped) with power from on high." (Luke 24:49 AMP) We literally put on the Holy Spirit of Jesus as we accept His saving grace by faith. Awaken to this fact that we are all free from the bondage of sin and the fear of eternal damnation by the grace of God!  God has made this happen because He is the great "I AM" (Exodus 3:14)  My people will know My Name!

What bondage are you still being chained up to?  Are you chained to alcohol? Are you chained to drugs, to sexual immorality, to greed, to jealousy? Perhaps you are just holding something against someone who wronged you in the past?  We all need to realize that by surrendering our lives to Jesus Christ, and accepting His grace through faith, we are given the power of the Holy Spirit. This new power within us makes wanting to be more like Jesus the deepest desire of our hearts. We want to please God more than we want alcohol, drugs, or any immorality. We want it more than any sinful desire that could be holding us down. We realize that God is the God who can do the impossible and release us from anything that is holding us down. All we need to do is surrender and pray. Let's go deeper and look at an example from the broadcast.



After Jesus is taken up to Heaven. The Disciples are given the Holy Spirit (Acts Chapter 2). While having some initial success with adding great numbers to the body of believers, the government and the religious leaders were starting to pursecute them with horrible acts. By Chapter 12, King Herod had come against the early believers by killing the Apostle James, the brother of John. Herod had also captured Peter and had Peter chained down in prison between Roman Guards. The entire church was praying for a miracle. Herod was planning to kill Peter the next day when we read:" [6] The very night before Herod was to bring him forward, Peter was sleeping between two soldiers, bound with two chains, and sentries were in front of the door guarding the prison. [7] Suddenly, an angel of the Lord appeared [beside him] and a light shone in the cell. The angel struck Peter's side and awakened him, saying, "Get up quickly!" And the chains fell off his hands. [8] The angel said to him, "Prepare yourself and strap on your sandals [to get ready for whatever may happen]." And he did so. Then the angel told him, "Put on your robe and follow me." (Acts 12:6-8 AMP)  From there, Peter walks out of the prison without any of the guards noticing him and joins the prayer meeting!

Peter was asleep thinking his life was over. The powers of the world had him chained down in what looked like a hopeless situation. But God, "Wonderful Counselor," "Mighty God," "Everlasting Father," "Prince of Peace" (Is 9:6), had another plan for Peter's life. Peter had much more to do to give God glory!

Whatever has you asleep, whatever has you in ragedy clothes and dirty from this world, whatever has you chained down; it has no power greater than the power of God within you as a believer in Jesus! Awaken, put on your beautiful gaments, and call upon the name of The Lord. My people will know My Name.

*May the peace and love of Christ be with you always!*

# WORDS OF WATER No. 14

"He who believes in Me [who adheres to, trusts in, and relies on Me], as the Scripture has said, 'From his innermost being will flow continually rivers of living water.'" —John 7:38

(For Further Study)

## *My People Will Know My Name*

Main Texts: Isaiah 52:6; Ex 20:7

Ever wonder why God wants us to know His Name?  The reason is quite simple, He wants us to appreciate, to the best of our human ability, all His many attributes (give Him glory). It is so important to God that He made the third commandment: 7 "You shall not take the name of the Lord your God in vain [that is, irreverently, in false

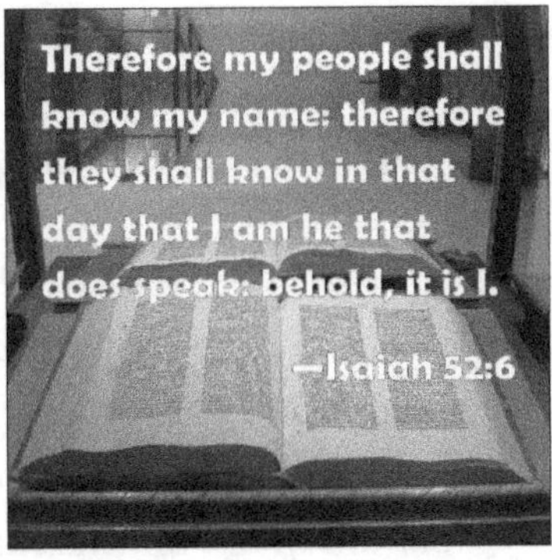


affirmations or in ways that impugn the character of God]; for the Lord will not hold guiltless nor leave unpunished the one who [b]takes His name in vain [disregarding its reverence and its power]." (Exodus 20:7 AMP)

Below, for our collective reference are some of the names for God used in the Old Testament and how many times each is used. The English Language is quite limited when it translates each of these to "God" or "Lord." So, please take a moment and reflect on each of these names for God below, and as you speak each one out loud, just pause and think about how limitless God really is…

- Elohim (God) <Gen 1:1 Used 2,599>
- Yahweh (Lord, Jehovah) <Gen 2:4 Used 6,519
- El Elyon (The Most High God) <Gen 14:18 Used 52>
- Adonai (Lord, Master) <Gen 15:2 Used 434>
- El Shaddai (Lord God Almighty) <Gen 17:1 Used 171>
- El Olam (The Everlasting God) <Gen 21:33 Used 439>

44

- Jehovah Jireh (The LORD Will Provide) <Gen 22:14 Used 1>
- Jehovah Rapha (The LORD Who Heals You) <Ex 15:26 Used 1>
- Jehovah Nissi (The LORD Is My Banner) <Ex 17:15 Used 1>
- El Qanna (Jealous God) <Ex 20:5 Used 6>
- Jehovah Mekoddishkem (The LORD Who Sanctifies You) <Ex31:13 Used 2>
- Jehovah Shalom (The LORD Is Peace) <Judges 6:24 Used 1>
- Jehovah Sabaoth (The LORD of Hosts) <1 Sam 1:3 Used 285>
- Jehovah Raah (The LORD Is My Shepherd) <Gen 48:15/PS 23:1 Used 4>
- Jehovah Tsidkenu (The LORD Our Righteousness) <Jer 23:6 Used 2>
- Jehovah Shammah (The LORD Is There) <Eziek 48:35 Used 1>

Have we discovered each of these aspects of God? Perhaps spending time looking up one or two of the references above will help each of us expand our knowledge and appreciation of God?

And of course, through one of the incomprehensible mysteries to mankind; the Father and the Son, and the Holy spirit, are all one

BEING. While Jesus was praying in the garden, just before offering up His life to pay for all our sins, He prayed: "I am no longer in the world; yet they are still in the world, and I am coming to You. Holy Father, keep them in Your name, the name which You have given Me, so that they may be one just as We are." (John 17:11 AMP)  The graphic at left portrays the names of Jesus from the New Testament like a Christmas Tree. Perhaps reflecting on all these names for Jesus will bless us as we give glory to Him as God.

Finally, we want to recognize the third aspect of the Trinity, The Holy Spirit. On the page below are over 30 more references for names of The Holy Spirit in Scripture.

God wants us to know Him intimately. He is not completely knowable by our limited human capabilities, but when we start reflecting upon His names throughout scripture, we can start to appreciate and give glory to all that He is, which is the glory due His name!

*May the peace and love of Christ be with you always!*

## Titles and names of the Holy Spirit

- Breath of the Almighty
  Job 33:4
- Comforter
  John 14:16 John 14:26 ; 15:26
- Eternal Spirit
  Hebrews 9:14
- Free Spirit
  Psalms 51:12
- God
  Acts 5:3 Acts 5:4
- Good Spirit
  Nehemiah 9:20 ; Psalms 143:10
- Holy Spirit
  Psalms 51:11 ; Luke 11:13 ; Ephesians 1:13 ; 4:30
- Lord, The
  2 Thessalonians 3:5
- Power of the Highest
  Luke 1:35

- Spirit, The
  Matthew 4:1 ; John 3:6 ; 1 Timothy 4:1
- Spirit of the Lord God
  Isaiah 61:1
- Spirit of the Lord
  Isaiah 11:2 ; Acts 5:9
- Spirit of God
  Genesis 1:2 ; 1 Corinthians 2:11 ; Job 33:4
- Spirit of the Father
  Matthew 10:20
- Spirit of Christ
  Romans 8:9 ; 1 Peter 1:11
- Spirit of the Son
  Galatians 4:6
- Spirit of life
  Romans 8:2 ; Revelation 11:11
- Spirit of grace
  Zechariah 12:10 ; Hebrews 10:29
- Spirit of prophecy
  Revelation 19:10
- Spirit of adoption
  Romans 8:15
- Spirit of wisdom
  Isaiah 11:2 ; Ephesians 1:17
- Spirit of counsel
  Isaiah 11:2
- Spirit of might
  Isaiah 11:2
- Spirit of understanding
  Isaiah 11:2
- Spirit of knowledge
  Isaiah 11:2
- Spirit of the fear of the Lord
  Isaiah 11:2
- Spirit of truth
  John 14:17 ; 15:26
- Spirit of holiness
  Romans 1:4
- Spirit of revelation
  Ephesians 1:17

- Spirit of judgment
  Isaiah 4:4 ; 28:6
- Spirit of burning
  Isaiah 4:4
- Spirit of glory
  1 Peter 4:14
- Seven Spirits of God
  Revelation 1:4

"He who believes in Me [who adheres to, trusts in, and relies on Me], as the Scripture has said, 'From his innermost being will flow continually rivers of living water.'" —John 7:38

## *Breaking away from the spirit of luck*
Main Texts: Ephesians 2:10; Luke 15:17-20; Psalm 1:1

How are you spending your Father's inheritance?  Have you thought about it much?  Or perhaps, you are just wondering through life counting on your own luck? Are you squandering your means? Are you listening to those voices in your head telling you that you are just "unlucky"?

Of course, we are talking today about our Heavenly Father, God Almighty, and our inheritance in the perspective of being His adopted child. When we accept the saving grace of salvation through Jesus, we are adopted into the Family of God. We are assured that we have all the means we need. Our Heavenly Father has a fullness of life (John 10:10) that is

> But as many as received him, to them gave he power to become the sons of God, even to them that believe on his name:
>
> —John 1:12

designed to give Him glory through the works He has planned for us: "10 For we are His workmanship [His own master work, a work of art], created in Christ Jesus [reborn from above—spiritually transformed, renewed, ready to be used] for good works, which God prepared [for us] beforehand [taking paths which He set], so that we would walk in them [living the good life which He prearranged and made ready for us]." (Ephesians 2:10 AMP)

But some believers do not understand what God has planned for them. Some do not stay close to God and they venture off, or backslide, into the world. Jesus told all of us a parable to help explain this situation and to warn us about relying on our own reasoning (the spirit of luck) in the Gospel of Luke, Chapter 15. The younger of the two sons is quite familiar with his father's estate. Instead of staying close to his father and enjoying the family fellowship, he decides to take an early payout and live life by his own direction, relying on his own luck to see him through. He spends his wealth, the blessings from his father, on prodigal living, which means extravagant parties and sinful appetites. There is a famine in the area he is living in and he ends up with a job feeding a farmer's pigs. The food for the pigs starts to look very good compared to what he can afford to feed himself. He is at the lowest of low points in his life. He has relied on his own luck and the world has taken everything from him and left him trying to eat as well as pigs!

Before we rush to judge this young man, we all need to be sure we have taken a hard look at our own situation. John warned all the early believers when he wrote: "[16] For all that is in the world—the lust and sensual craving of the flesh and the lust and longing of the eyes and the boastful pride of life [pretentious confidence in one's resources or in the

stability of earthly things]—these do not come from the Father, but are from the world." (1 John 2:16 AMP) The pretentious confidence is the spirit of luck in today's message. We must break away from this spirit, but how do we do that exactly? Let's return to Jesus' teaching…

We see in Luke 15:17-18 AMP, "[17] But when he [finally] came to his senses, he said, 'How many of my father's hired men have more than enough food, while I am dying here of hunger! [18] I will get up and go to my father, and I will say to him, "Father, I have sinned against heaven and in your sight." Do you see the two simple things we all need to do to break away from the spirit of luck?

First, we need to remember who our Father really is. We need to remember that God is Almighty, All-Powerful, Everlasting, Creator, Provider, Protector, Lord of Lords and King of Kings! This young man first remembered how his father was providing for everyone in the household, servants and siblings alike! Go back and re-read the quotation from Ephesians 2 above – we are all works of art in the eyes of God!

The second requirement for breaking the spirit of luck is sincere repentance. The young man knew he had sinned because the Holy Spirit convicts every child of God when we are disobedient. Thankfully, we are washed clean by the blood of Jesus: "If we [freely] admit that we have sinned and confess our sins, He is faithful and just [true to His own nature and promises], and will forgive our sins and cleanse us continually from all unrighteousness [our wrongdoing, everything not in conformity with His will and purpose]." (1 John 1:9 AMP)

If we find ourselves wondering out in the world, squandering the life God has for us, we need to break away from the spirit of luck by remembering who God really is and repenting with a humble and sincere heart!  How will God react when we break away from the spirit of luck? Let's look at the way Jesus describes the scene: "[20] So he got up and came to his father. But while he was still a long way off, his father saw him and was moved with compassion for him, and ran and embraced him and kissed him." (Luke 15:20 AMP). Our Heavenly Father longs to embrace each of His children when they come back home to Him! Break away from the spirit of luck today!

*May the peace and love of Christ be with you always!*

"He who believes in Me [who adheres to, trusts in, and relies on Me], as the Scripture has said, 'From his innermost being will flow continually rivers of living water.'" —John 7:38

(For Further Study)

## *Breaking away from the spirit of luck*

Main Texts: *Luke15:17-20; John 14:2; Ephesians 5:6-10*

Remember the first time you came back home after a long trip, or being away for the first time on your own?  Remember how nice it felt to be in familiar surroundings – the sights, the smells, the memories? There is a special peace that comes from being where you know you belong.

In today's broadcast, we explored the experience of a young man who ventured away from his home, the home of his father, and relied on the spirit of luck (that thinking of "I will just take my chances" or worse, "I will work things out for myself"). It did not go well for this young man. He eventually came to his senses, repented of his sins, and returned to the loving arms of his father. (Luke 15:17-20). Jesus told this story so that we would always have a reminder of where we belong and what awaits us at our true home.

For every believer, Jesus has paid the price for sin and enabled us to enter our true spiritual home someday in heaven. We are told our home town will be one of many "mansions" (John 14:2) and beyond anything we can possibly imagine as a mere human.



But we do not have to wait until heaven to start experiencing the peace of being where we belong!  Paul reminded the Corinthians that God actually sets up His home inside of each believer:" 19Do you not know that your body is a temple of the Holy Spirit who is within you, whom you have [received as a gift] from God, and that you are not your own [property]? 20You were bought with a price [you were actually purchased with the precious blood of Jesus and made His own]. So then, honor and glorify God with your body." (1 Corinthians 6:19-20). God wants to make each of us feel at home with Him constantly. We do this when we break away from the spirit of luck and obey the promptings of the Holy Spirit towards the works God has planned for us before time began!

Of course, the world, the spirit of luck, yells to us that we will miss out on the "pleasures of life" if we do not pursue our sinful desires. These yells come through movies, television shows/ commercials, even social media. Jesus' half-brother James, wrote a stern warning to the early believers that certainly applies today: " 13 Let no one say when he is tempted, "I am being tempted by God" [for temptation does not originate from God, but from our own flaws]; for God cannot be tempted by [what is] evil, and He Himself tempts no one. 14 But each one is tempted when he is dragged away, enticed and baited [to commit sin] by his own [worldly] desire (lust, passion)." (James 1:12-14 AMP) Only by breaking away from the spirit of luck can we experience the life Jesus has called us to live.

Paul, this time to the group of early believers in the town of Ephesus warned: "6 Let no one deceive you with empty arguments [that encourage you to sin], for because of these things the wrath of God comes upon the sons of disobedience [those who habitually sin]. 7 So do not participate or even associate with them [in the rebelliousness of sin]. 8 For once you were darkness, but now you are light in the Lord; walk as children of Light [live as those who are native-born to the Light] 9 (for the fruit [the effect, the result] of the Light consists in all goodness and righteousness and truth), 10 trying to learn [by experience] what is pleasing to the Lord [and letting your lifestyles be examples of what is most acceptable to Him—your behavior expressing gratitude to God for your salvation]." (Ephesians 5:6-10 AMP)

Jesus described himself as the Good Shepherd who controls the door to the pastures of life. He longs to have us stay home where we belong, with Him. He even tells us in explicit terms what he wants to

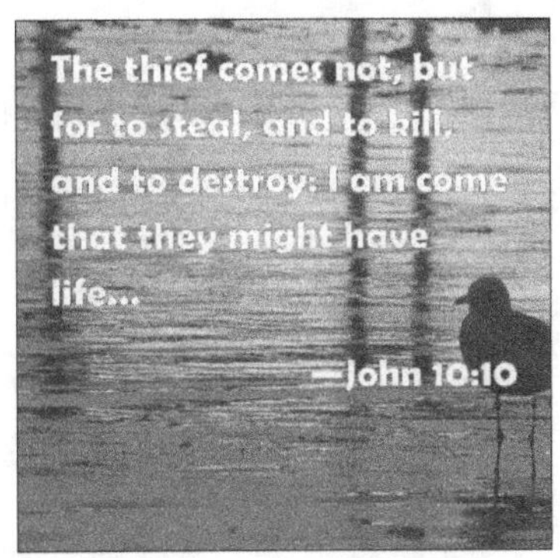


provide for us: " 9 I am the Door; anyone who enters through Me will be saved [and will live forever], and will go in and out [freely], and find pasture (spiritual security). 10 The thief comes only in order to steal and kill and destroy. I came that they may have and enjoy life, and have it in abundance [to the full, till it overflows]." (John 10:9-10 AMP) This is why we must break away from the spirit of luck – it is the secret to living the life Jesus wants to live through us. His Spirit wants to be at home in us so we can feel at home and live out life to its fullest – as Jesus defines it – which is so much better than anything the spirit of luck can ever promise. The spirit of luck wants to steal our joy, kill our hope, and destroy the Kingdom Works of God through us. Break away from the spirit of luck and come back home today!

May the peace and love of Christ be with you always!

# WORDS OF WATER No. 17

"He who believes in Me [who adheres to, trusts in, and relies on Me], as the Scripture has said, 'From his innermost being will flow continually rivers of living water.'" —John 7:38

(For Further Study)
## *Breaking away from the spirit of luck*

Main Texts: Luke15:17-20; John 14:2; Ezekiel 36:26-27
Galatians 5:19-24

This broadcast was all about breaking away from the spirit of luck, or the pull of the world to throw away what is true and "take our chances" pursing worldly desires. The primary illustration is "The Prodigal Son" found in Luke 15. We have looked at why we must return home to God our Father, but today we are going to go deeper into how we know we have broken away from the spirit of luck.

The first key point that we all need to remember is that God has already given us EVERYTHING we need to break away from the spirit of luck! God does not rely on anything human to help us. He knows we are fallen creatures with no way to right our situation before His perfect holiness (Romans 3:22-24). There is no way we can restore our relationship to Him unless He makes that way possible. The good news, the Gospel, is that our gracious God has paid our sin debt in full! So, our first step in breaking the spirit of luck is to just accept the free gift of SALVATION through Gods grace in the sacrifice of Himself on the cross.

For by grace are you saved through faith; and that not of yourselves: it is the gift of God:

—Ephesians 2:8

But God is not finished with our lives once we accept Jesus as Savior. God wants to transform each of us into the same kind of person that Jesus exemplified when He walked the Earth in human form. God needs us transformed so we will do His will – the works He has for us. The purpose we were created to fulfill. What might even be more amazing, is that nearly 600 years before Jesus arrived, through the Prophet Ezekiel, God made a new promise to humans: "[26] Moreover, I will give you a new heart and put a new spirit within you, and I will remove the heart of stone from your flesh and give you a heart of flesh. [27] I will put My Spirit within you and cause you to walk in My Statutes, and you will keep My Ordinances and do them." (Ezekiel 36:26-27 AMP) Not only does God provide full payment of our sin debt, but He gives us a new heart, a new spirit!

The Prodigal Son "came to his senses" (Luke 15:17) and repented. We too, need to allow the Holy Spirit that lives within us to eliminate our fears, unleash the power to resist the temptations of this world, to love God and others as ourselves, and be at peace. (2 Timothy 1:7)

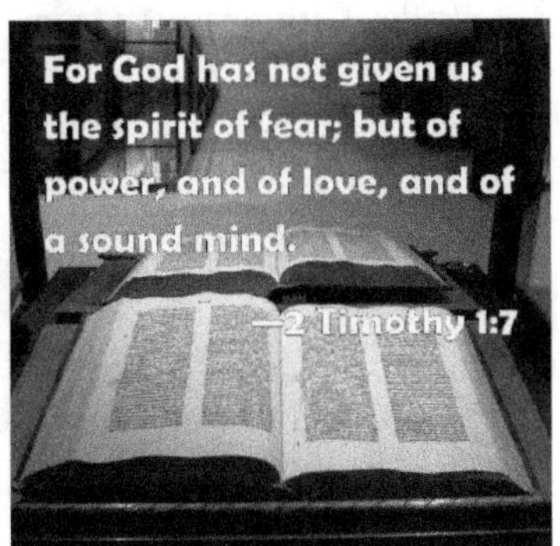


It is easy to know when we have broken away from the spirit of luck. We need only to turn to Paul's letter to the early believers, in the area of Galacia, to get a definitive list of contrasting behavors between those operating their lives under the spirit of luck verses those operating under the Holy Spirit: "[19] Now the practices of the [i]sinful nature are clearly evident: they are sexual immorality, impurity, sensuality (total irresponsibility, lack of self-control), [20] [j]idolatry, [k]sorcery, hostility, strife, jealousy, fits of anger, disputes, dissensions, factions [that promote heresies], [21] envy, drunkenness, riotous behavior, and other things like these. I warn you beforehand, just as I did previously, that those who practice such things will not inherit the kingdom of God. [22] But the fruit of the Spirit [the result of His presence within us] is love [unselfish concern for others], joy, [inner] peace, patience [not the ability to wait, but how we act while waiting], kindness, goodness, faithfulness, [23] gentleness, self-control. Against such things there is no law. [24] And those who belong to Christ Jesus have crucified the [l]sinful nature together with its passions and appetites." (Galatians 5:19-24 AMP)

If you are "taking your chances" and operating your life under the worldly standards we all witness so frequently, come to your senses! First, accept God's free gift of salvation by grace through faith in Jesus. Then know that God has placed a new spirit, His Holy Spirit, within you to bring you the sweet fruits of a full life. Break away from the spirit of luck by remembering what God has done for you, telling God you are sorry for any sins, and that you want His Spirit to transform you into the person, more like Jesus, He created you to be. We can all live lives full of love, joy, peace, patience, kindness, goodness, and faithfulness. Praise be to God!

*May the peace and love of Christ be with you always!*

"He who believes in Me [who adheres to, trusts in, and relies on Me], as the Scripture has said, 'From his innermost being will flow continually rivers of living water.'" —John 7:38

## *Come to God for Safety*

Main Texts: Psalm 91:1-3; John 14:23; Luke 6:46-48

Everywhere we turn in our world today there is fear, anxiety, and worry. It seems like there is no place that is safe. But as believers in Jesus, we do have a place we can go. We can come to God for safety!

Once we believe that God has paid our sin debt in full through the sacrifice Jesus made in our place, we are adopted into the family of God: [26] For you [who are born-again have been reborn from above—spiritually transformed, renewed, sanctified and] are all children of God [set apart for His purpose with full rights and privileges] through faith in Christ Jesus.

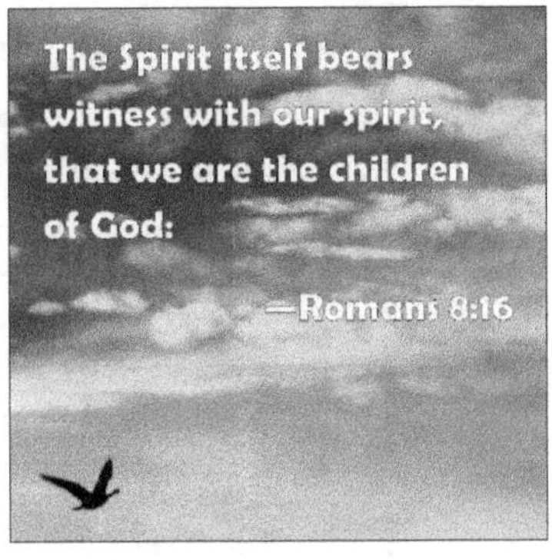


(Galatians 3:26 AMP) As any good father provides shelter and protection for his family, our Heavenly Father promises us safety when we come to Him: "He who [a]dwells in the shelter of the Most High will remain secure and rest in the shadow of the Almighty [whose power no enemy can withstand]." (Psalm 91:1 AMP)

While this is comforting, some may be wondering how can we find this dwelling?  Well God is not talking about living in the church building, so where is His dwelling?  As always, Jesus gives us the answers to these questions. In the Gospel of John, Jesus was talking about this topic, "[23] Jesus answered, "If anyone [really] loves Me, he will keep My word (teaching); and My Father will love him, and We will come to him and make Our dwelling place with him. (John 14:23 AMP). The dwelling place is inside of us!  And before we start to worry about trying to remember everything Jesus said (His teaching), Jesus goes on to explain that He has given us a Helper, "26 But the [d]Helper (Comforter, Advocate, Intercessor—Counselor, Strengthener, Standby), the Holy Spirit, whom the Father will send in My name [in My place, to represent Me and act on My behalf], He will teach you all things. And He will help you remember everything that I have told you. 27 Peace I leave with you; My [perfect] peace I give to you; not as the world gives do I give to you. Do not let your heart be troubled, nor let it be afraid. [Let My perfect peace calm you in every circumstance and give you courage and strength for every challenge.] (John 14:26-27 AMP). We need to read our Bibles with meditation and prayer. We need to stop when we feel that prompting of The Holy Spirit and ask, "What are You telling me Lord?." Then we need to trust and rely on God to reveal Himself and what He wants us to know.

We have the safety, and peace of mind, promised by God through the working of the Holy Spirit inside us. We simply come out of the world by surrendering our sinful selves to the power of the Holy Spirit, Who helps us dwell in the Words of Jesus and in response God (Father, Son, and Spirit) turns us into their dwelling, where there is ultimate safety. Just look at the rest of the promise in Psalm 91:

2I will say of the Lord, "He is my refuge and my fortress,
My God, in whom I trust [with great confidence, and on whom I rely]!"
3 For He will save you from the trap of the fowler,
And from the deadly pestilence.
4 He will cover you and completely protect you with His pinions,
And under His wings you will find refuge;
His faithfulness is a shield and a wall. (Psalm 91:2-4)

But this promise is conditional on trusting God and allowing ourselves to be led by the Holy Spirit in obedience. Jesus warned all of His followers about how to build a strong dwelling for safety:[46] "Why do you call Me, 'Lord, Lord,' and do not practice what I tell you? [47] Everyone who comes to Me and listens to My words and obeys them, I will show you whom he is like: [48] he is like a [far-sighted, practical, and sensible] man building a house, who dug deep and laid a foundation on the rock; and when a flood occurred, the torrent burst against that house and yet could not shake it, because it had been securely built and founded on the rock. (Luke 6:46-48 AMP) We need only to trust and obey Jesus to have the safety of a fortress built upon the rock of Jesus Himself. Come to God for Safety Today!

*May the peace and love of Christ be with you always!*

"He who believes in Me [who adheres to, trusts in, and relies on Me], as the Scripture has said, 'From his innermost being will flow continually rivers of living water.'" —John 7:38

## *What are you doing with your freedom?*

Main Texts: Exodus 9:1; II Chronicles 7:16; Luke 4:16-20

There are two aspects of "freedom," one positive and one negative. The negative aspect of freedom is most often discussed. This is the aspect of being freed, or gaining freedom FROM something negative, like slavery, oppression, injustice. But the positive aspect of freedom must also be considered. This is the aspect of being freed or gaining the ability to MOVE TOWARDS something else. God wants us all to consider, and act upon, both aspects of freedom in our lives as believers. What are you doing with your freedom?

The good news, or The Gospel, of Jesus the Christ has both aspects of freedom. We are released from the un-payable debts our sins represent before a Holy, Just, and Perfect God when we simply accept the gracious gift God offers to everyone by the death and resurrection of Jesus! There is nothing we can do to obligate God to set us free. Only by His grace and His mercy we are freed from the power of sin and we need only to accept this by faith. Jesus proclaimed this good news when He was preaching His first public sermon recorded in the Gospel of Luke:

[16] So He came to Nazareth, where He had been brought up; and as was His custom, He entered the synagogue on the Sabbath, and stood up to read. [17] The scroll of the prophet Isaiah was handed to Him. He unrolled the scroll and found the place where it was written, [18] "The Spirit of the Lord is

upon Me (the Messiah), Because He has anointed Me to preach the good news to the poor. He has sent Me to announce release (pardon, forgiveness) to the captives, And recovery of sight to the blind, To set free those who are oppressed (downtrodden, bruised, crushed by tragedy),[19] to proclaim the favorable year of the Lord [the day when salvation and the favor of God abound greatly]." [20] Then He rolled up the scroll [having stopped in the middle of the verse], gave it back to the attendant and sat down [to teach]; and the eyes of all those in the synagogue were [attentively] fixed on Him. [21] He began speaking to them: "Today this Scripture has been fulfilled in your hearing and in your presence." (Luke 4:16-20 AMP)

But this freedom from sin is only half of the total freedom we experience with God. God wants us to use our freedom to MOVE TOWARDS serving Him. We know this from what He told Moses in the book of Exodus: [1] Then the Lord said to Moses, "Go to Pharaoh and tell him, 'Thus says the Lord, the God of the Hebrews: "Let My people go, so that they may serve Me. (Exodus 9:1 AMP). God gave the Israelites their freedom from Pharaoh not only to be freed from the bondage and slavery but also that they could be free to serve Him!  He expects all of us to do the same. What are you doing with your freedom?

Perhaps we all need some reminders on what "serving God" looks like?  First, service looks like worship. When we realize we are freed from the bondage and slavery of sin, we are free to worship and give thanks to God for His graciousness and mercy. Next, we see ourselves as humbled but confident vessels of The Holy Spirit.

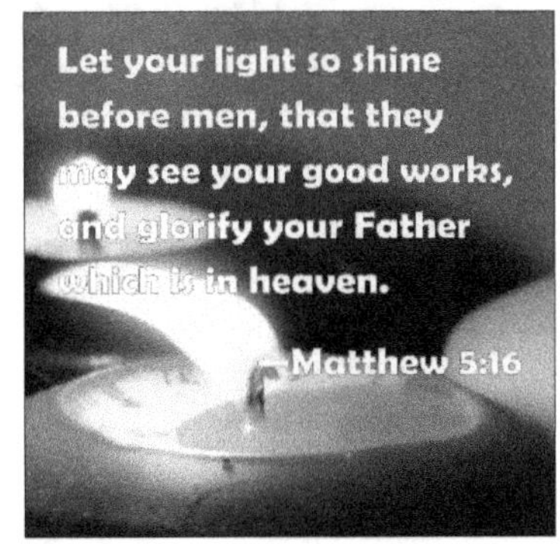


When Solomon was dedicating the physical Temple that had taken 40 plus years to build, God  told the people of Israel: [16] "For now I have chosen and sanctified and set apart for My purpose this house that My

Name may be here forever, and My eyes and My heart will be here perpetually." (II Chronicles 7:16) That temple was destroyed because the people of God did not follow His ways and gave up their freedoms. In the New Covenant, God makes His home in our hearts: [19] Do you not know that your body is a temple of the Holy Spirit who is within you, whom you have [received as a gift] from God, and that you are not your own [property]? [20] You were bought with a price [you were actually purchased with the precious blood of Jesus and made His own]. So then, honor and glorify God with your body. (1 Corinthians 6:19-20 AMP). We make the most of our freedom when we honor God with our service, our worship, and our humble surrender to His presence that leads us to good works that God has planned for us since before time.

What are you doing with your freedom? Are you reflecting upon the saving grace of the precious blood of Jesus that has freed you from the power of your sinful self and the bondage of those sins? Are you using your freedom to serve God by worshiping Him? Are you humbly moving towards the freedom of being a temple of the Holy Spirit to shine the light of Christ into this dark world? Break away from anything that is holding you down today and accept Jesus as your Savior and your Lord. Let The Holy Spirit lead you to the full life He has for you. Use your freedom for the glory of God!

*May the peace and love of Christ be with you always!*

"He who believes in Me [who adheres to, trusts in, and relies on Me], as the Scripture has said, 'From his innermost being will flow continually rivers of living water.'" —John 7:38

(For Further Study)

## *What are you doing with your freedom?*

Main Texts: Exodus 9:1; Exodus 24:7-8; John 8:31-37; Mark 5:20; Romans 6:16; Matthew 28:19

We are diving deeper into the freedom we have through the Gospel of Jesus the Christ. We learned that God set the Israelites free so that they could serve Him <Exodus 9:1>. We also know that a big part of this new freedom came with God's desire for His chosen people (Israel) to be obedient to His commandments <Exodus 22 – 24>, known as the Book of the Covenant:

[7] Then he (Moses) took the Book of the Covenant and read it aloud to the people; and they said, "Everything that the Lord has said we will do, and we will be obedient." [8] So Moses took the blood [which had been placed in the large basins] and sprinkled it on the people, and said, "Behold the blood of the covenant, which the Lord has made with you in accordance with all these words." (Exodus 24:7-8 AMP).

The story did not end there, however, and the people who said they would celebrate their freedom by serving God in obedience actually broke their covenant with God. So God, in His infinite grace and mercy, made a New Covenant with a new "chosen people." And this time He did not use the blood of animals to seal the promise. He used His own blood. He humbled Himself and came down out of Heaven in the form of a man to pay the price than no other man could pay. Jesus followed every commandment of the Old Testament/Old Covenant perfectly so that He could be that perfect sacrifice before a Holy God. His body and blood are now in us every time we remember Him through Communion. Jesus the Christ, has now established the New Covenant with all who accept Him by faith and follow Him in surrendered obedience.

Here are His words:

[31] So Jesus was saying to the Jews who had believed Him, "If you abide in My word [continually obeying My teachings and living in accordance with them, then] you are truly My disciples. [32] And you will know the truth [regarding salvation], and the truth will set you free [from the penalty of sin]." [33] They answered Him, "We are Abraham's descendants and have never been enslaved to anyone. [d]What do You mean by saying, 'You will be set free'?" [34] Jesus answered, "I assure you and most solemnly say to you, everyone who practices sin habitually is a slave of sin. [35] Now the slave does not remain in a household forever; the son [of the master] does remain forever. [36] So if the Son makes you free, then you are unquestionably free. [37] I know that you are Abraham's descendants; yet you plan to kill Me, because My word has no place [to grow] in you [and it makes no change in your heart]. John 8:31-37 AMP)

Jesus sets us free and offers us the opportunity to change our hearts. What are you doing with your freedom?

Let's look at two more examples or people who were set free by Jesus and what they did with their freedom. The first example is a man who was possessed by hundreds of demons. He was naked and hung out in the cemetery. Everyone in his region knew of him and how insane he was. Can you imaging being held captive by over a hundred demons at the same time?  Maybe you are in bondage from the demon of addiction. Maybe you are in bondage from the demon of lust. Maybe you are in bondage from the demons of greed, jealousy, anxiety, worry, physical infirmities. If your list sums to 100+, then you can certainly identify with this man. But for Jesus, there is no demon too powerful, and there is no group of demons that can resist His power. Jesus casts all the demons out of this man just like He will cast out any demon that has you in bondage!

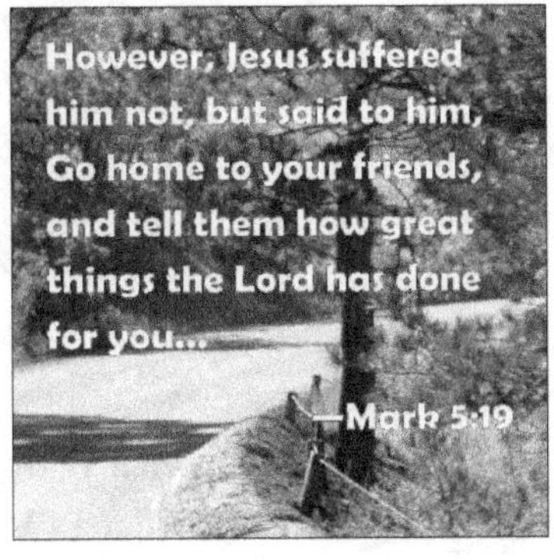


What did the man do with his new freedom?  He first asked to go with Jesus, but we learn how he was OBEDIENT to his new Lord: [19] Jesus did not let him [come], but [instead] He said to him, "Go home to your family and tell them all the great things that the Lord has done for you, and how He has had mercy on you." [20] So he [obeyed and] went away and began to publicly proclaim in Decapolis [the region of the ten Hellenistic cities] all the great things that Jesus had done for him; and all the people were astonished. (Mark 5:19-20 AMP)  This man used his freedom to serve God by spreading the good news of Jesus the Christ. What are you doing with your freedom?

The next example we will look at is a woman. This example is particularly insightful for several reasons: first, Jewish customs (not God's commandments) forbid a man alone to speak with a woman alone. Secondly, this woman was a Samaritan, which meant that she was part of the group that had intermarried with conquering peoples (Mesopotamia and Syria) and were no longer considered "Jewish." Think of them as a racially discriminated minority group at the time of Jesus. She was drawing water at a well in the middle of the day, which meant that she was also an outcast from the other women who would have come to the well in the cool of the morning. This was because she had been part of four failed marriages and was living in sin with a fifth man. But notice The Savior's heart towards her. Jesus reveals His knowledge of her past and dismisses her concerns about the man-made customs they were breaking. He simply extends to her the same grace and mercy He extends to all those who believe in Him. He offers her "life giving water," which is Himself <John 4:14>. We then learn of her reaction to her new freedom: 28 Then the woman left her water jar, and went into the city and began telling the people, 29 "Come, see a man who told me all the things that I have done! Can this be the Christ (the Messiah, the Anointed)?" 30 So the people left the city and were coming to Him. (John 4:28-30 AMP)   She used her new freedom to serve God by telling everyone in her town that she had found the Messiah!  What are you doing with your freedom?

We have choices. We can choose to continue to be slaves or we can choose to be free. We can choose to accept the grace by faith that God offers or stay in bondage to sin. Either choice leads to obedience as Paul warned the Romans: 16 Do you not know that when you continually offer yourselves to someone to do his will, you are the slaves of the one whom you obey, either [slaves] of sin, which leads to death, or of obedience, which leads to righteousness (right standing with God)? (Romans 6:16 AMP).

Jesus makes it very clear through the examples above and His last directions to all His followers before He went back up to Heaven:19 Go therefore and make disciples of all the nations [help the people to learn of Me, believe in Me, and obey My words], baptizing them in the name of the Father and of the Son and of the Holy



Spirit, 20 teaching them to observe everything that I have commanded you; and lo, I am with you always [remaining with you perpetually—regardless of circumstance, and on every occasion], even to the end of the age." (Matthew 28:19-20 AMP)   What are you doing with your freedom?


*May the peace and love of Christ be with you always!*

"He who believes in Me [who adheres to, trusts in, and relies on Me], as the Scripture has said, 'From his innermost being will flow continually rivers of living water.'" —John 7:38

## *Jesus is The Way!*

Main Texts: John 14:1-6; Ephesians 3:16-20

Are you desperate even to the point of ending your life? Are you questioning and second-guessing all the big decisions in your life to date? Are people avoiding you? Perhaps you just feel completely lost and do not know which way to go? We have great news – there is a clear way, there is a lighted pathway, there is a beacon of hope ahead of you – His name is Jesus!

Jesus is the Christ, the perfect sacrifice made for all mankind to reconcile us to a Holy God. And because He made that sacrifice, we know "the way." Jesus told His doubting Disciple Thomas, and all of His followers afterwards, very plainly: [1]"Do not let your heart be troubled (afraid, cowardly). Believe [confidently] in God and trust in Him, [have faith, hold on to it, rely on it, keep going and] believe also in Me.

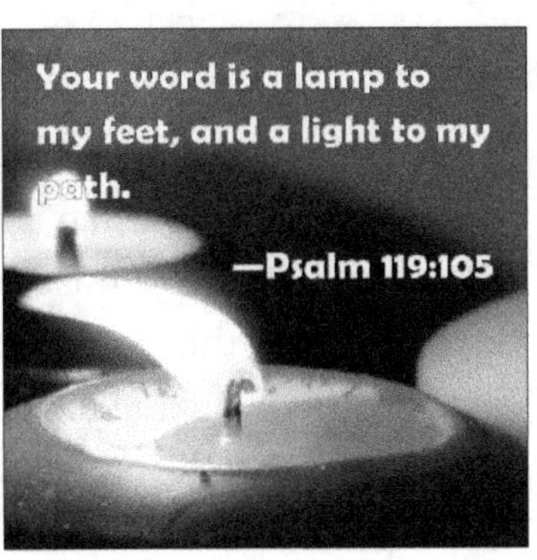


[2] In My Father's house are many dwelling places. If it were not so, I would have told you, because I am going there to prepare a place for you. [3] And if I go and prepare a place for you, I will come back again and I will take you to Myself, so that where I am you may be also. [4] And [to the place] where I am going, you know the way." [5] Thomas said to Him, "Lord, we do not know where You are going; so how can we know the way?" [6] Jesus said to him, "[a]I am the [only] Way [to God] and the [real] Truth and the [real] Life; no one comes to the Father but through Me. (John 14:1-6 AMP) We now know the way to Heaven is with/through Jesus and that should give us great joy. But Jesus also provided us with clear

directions for navigating life until we get to Heaven – and the way is still with/through Him. Jesus is the way!

Jesus knows everything because He is God, along with The Father and Spirit. He knows we are still living in a fallen world. So he has given us several promises to rely on for navigating our way through life. He promises to light our way: [12] Once more Jesus addressed the crowd. He said, "[a]I am the Light of the world. He who follows Me will not walk in the darkness, but will have the Light of life. (John 8:12 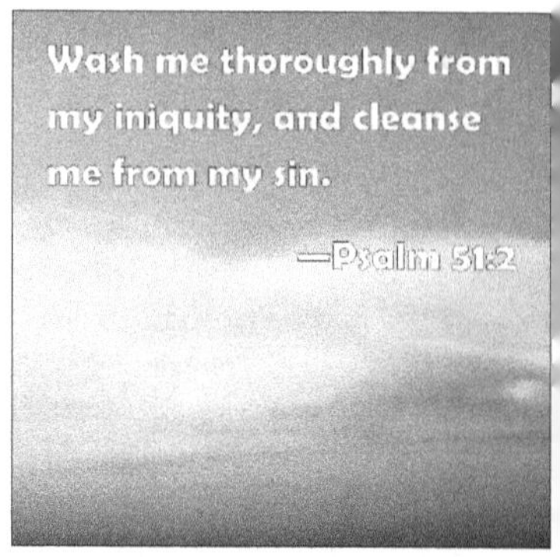
AMP) Jesus offers to pace our life and carry our burdens: [28] "Come to Me, all who are weary and heavily burdened [by religious rituals that provide no peace], and I will give you rest [refreshing your souls with salvation]. [29] Take My yoke upon you and learn from Me [following Me as My disciple], for I am gentle and humble in heart, and you will find rest (renewal, blessed quiet) for your souls. [30] For My yoke is easy [to bear] and My burden is light." Jesus even tells us that the reason He has told us these promises is so we can have peace of mind: "I have told you these things, so that in Me you may have [perfect] peace. In the world you have tribulation and distress and suffering, but be courageous [be confident, be undaunted, be filled with joy]; I have overcome the world." [My conquest is accomplished, My victory abiding.] (John 16:33 AMP) Jesus is the way!

Maybe you are wondering how you find Jesus and how He then directs your ways as depicted above? The answer could not be simpler. We need only to drink Him in like water – invite Him to live in our heart and be our Lord and Savior. Once we accept Him into our hearts, His Holy Spirit Power resides within us and through His Word, Prayer, Meditation, Fasting, and Fellowship with other believers He guides us and fulfills His promises.

Our prayers for you are the same as those prayed by Paul to the early believers in Ephesus:

[16] May He grant you out of the riches of His glory, to be strengthened and spiritually energized with power through His Spirit in your inner self, [indwelling your innermost being and personality], [17] so that Christ may dwell in your hearts through your faith. And may you, having been [deeply] rooted and [securely] grounded in love, [18] be fully capable of comprehending with all the saints (God's people) the width and length and height and depth of His love [fully experiencing that amazing, endless love]; [19] and [that you may come] to know [practically, through personal experience] the love of Christ which far surpasses [mere] knowledge [without experience], that you may be filled up [throughout your being] to all the fullness of God [so that you may have the richest experience of God's presence in your lives, completely filled and flooded with God Himself]. [20] Now to Him who is able to [carry out His purpose and] do superabundantly more than all that we dare ask or think [infinitely beyond our greatest prayers, hopes, or dreams], according to His power that is at work within us, 21 to Him be the glory in the church and in Christ Jesus throughout all generations forever and ever. Amen. (Ephesians 3:16-20 AMP) **Jesus is the way!**

*May the peace and love of Christ be with you always*

"He who believes in Me [who adheres to, trusts in, and relies on Me], as the Scripture has said, 'From his innermost being will flow continually rivers of living water.'" —John 7:38

## *Jesus is The Way!*

Main Texts: John 14:1-6; Ephesians 3:16-20

*There are two interpretations of the English word "way."

Noun
1. A method style or manner of doing something
   "There are two ways of approaching this product"

| Similar | Method | Course of Action | Process | Procedure | Technique |
|---|---|---|---|---|---|

2. A road, track, path or street for traveling along.
   "No. 3 Church Way"

Last time we explored how Jesus is the way from the perspective of the second meaning – Jesus being the pathway to The Father in Heaven. We know that because Jesus paid our sin debt with His precious, holy, and perfect blood, those who believe are forgiven of sin by grace through faith. We have done nothing deserving of this free gift, it is purely by God's grace that we have this pathway. Jesus is the way!

We next want to explore the other meaning – that of "a method or style of doing something." The "something" we are referring to is life. How do we do life? What methods do we follow? How would others describe our "style" as they see us go through life?

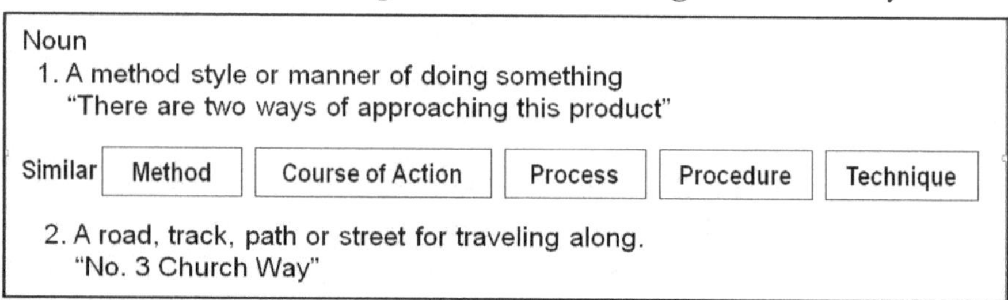


Jesus taught us everything we need to know about doing life. Part of these teachings are recorded in John's Gospel, the 15th Chapter. Jesus begins that chapter by explaining how to connect with Him so that we can be sure we are utilizing His methods and His style: 1"I am the true Vine, and My Father is the vinedresser. 2 Every branch in Me that does not bear fruit, He takes away; and every branch that continues to bear fruit, He [repeatedly] prunes, so that it will bear more fruit [even richer and finer fruit]. 3 You are already clean because of the word which I have given you [the teachings which I have discussed with you]. 4 Remain in Me, and I [will remain] in you. Just as no branch can bear fruit by itself without remaining in the vine, neither can you [bear fruit, producing evidence of your faith] unless you remain in Me. 5 I am the Vine; you are the branches. The one who remains in Me and I in him bears much fruit, for [otherwise] apart from Me [that is, cut off from vital union with Me] you can do nothing. (John 15:1-5 AMP) If we stay connected to Jesus, we have the freedom to branch out into life with confidence and boldness. Sure, there will be times or even seasons when we feel God's pruning. But God is just preparing us for bearing even more fruit!

We stay connected as a branch by staying in Jesus' teachings – The Word of God. In fact, Jesus makes it very clear that if we do get disconnected – if we try other methods or other styles, WE CAN DO NOTHING! This means that while we may look like we are doing something "good," if we are not acting out of the connection to Jesus, if our heart is not

aligned with His heart and that of The Father's – it is nothing. Jesus explained it further by saying: 8 "My Father is glorified and honored by this, when you bear much fruit, and prove yourselves to be My [true] disciples. 9 I have loved you just as the Father has loved Me; remain in My love [and do not doubt My love for you]. 10 If you keep My commandments and obey My teaching, you will remain in My love, just as I have kept My Father's commandments and remain in His love." (John 15:8 AMP) Jesus modeled the methods and style of life we should lead. Jesus is the way!

But how do we know if we are connected to Jesus? How do we know we are "bearing fruit"? What does this fruit look like? The Holy

Spirit inspired the Apostle Paul to write down the fruits of having the Spirit of Jesus, the Holy Spirit, guiding our lives: 22 "But the fruit of the Spirit [the result of His presence within us] is love [unselfish concern for others], joy, [inner] peace, patience [not the ability to wait, but how we act while waiting], kindness, goodness, faithfulness, 23 gentleness, self-control. Against such things there is no law. 24 And those who belong to Christ Jesus have crucified the sinful nature together with its passions and appetites. 25 If we [claim to] live by the [Holy] Spirit, we must also walk by the Spirit [with personal integrity, godly character, and moral courage—our conduct empowered by the Holy Spirit]. 26 We must not become conceited, challenging or provoking one another, envying one another." (Galatians 5:22-26 AMP) Are you longing to see these fruits in your own life? Spend some quiet time regularly listening to the words Jesus speaks and observing the way Jesus lived. Adopt His methods and His style for addressing every situation. Invite His Holy Spirit to guide you and lead you. Jesus is the way!

*May the peace and love of Christ be with you always!*

"He who believes in Me [who adheres to, trusts in, and relies on Me], as the Scripture has said, 'From his innermost being will flow continually rivers of living water.'" —John 7:38

## *Who has controlled history since the beginning?*

Main Texts: Isaiah 41:4; John 1:1-5

This broadcast has such an important message that it will be broken down into three successive parts. In answering this question, "Who has controlled history since the beginning?" we will first explore what God's Word reveals about "WHO," from the quotations above. Then in number 24 and 25 we will explore examples from the Bible of people that had their histories changed, and finally we will look at how Jesus invites all of us to se history in a new perspective.

The first answer of "Who has controlled history since the beginning?" is somewhat revealed in the word "history." It may be more obvious if we were to always write this word as "HIS-story." We need to constantly remind ourselves that it is not about us! Our existence, and what mankind has documented about events related to that existence, is really all about God. It is the Triune (3-in-one) and only God that has orchestrated everything – including defining time for humans. God (Father/Son/Spirit) existed before there was "time" and will exist after He determines "the end of time."

"Who has performed and done this, Calling forth [and guiding the destinies of] the generations [of the nations] from the beginning? 'I, the Lord—the first, and with the last [existing before history began, the ever-present, unchanging God]—I am He.'" (Isaiah 41:4 AMP)

So, if God was "before time," and He created time, He obviously did not "need" humans to exist as Himself. He did not need anything. He also does not need to explain everything about Himself, except what He chooses to reveal. A. W. Tozer wrote a classic book called, "The Knowledge Of The Holy" (NY, 1961) that explores many of the aspects of God which humans can only attempt to comprehend as part of God's created beings. But suffice it to say that God chose to create all of mankind and enter relationship with us: [26] Then God said, "Let Us (Father, Son, Holy Spirit) make man in Our image, according to Our likeness [not physical, but a spiritual personality and moral likeness]; and let them have complete authority over the fish of the sea, the birds of the air, the cattle, and over the entire earth, and over everything that creeps and crawls on the earth." [27] So God created man in His own image, in the image and likeness of God He created him; male and female He created them. (Genesis 1:26-27 AMP) God is the One who has controlled history since the beginning!

God had a specific purpose and mission for every aspect of His creation, including mankind. He wanted to share the glory of His perfect love. He also gave some of the higher beings of His creation (Angels and Humans specifically) a choice to join in that love relationship that Father/Son/Spirit had been enjoying before time. God is all-knowing, so He already knew there would be some created beings that would try and be their own gods. In giving them a choice, some would allow pride to cause sin and separation from God. In His perfect justice and infinite mercy and infinite grace, however, God had already made accommodations (before time) for the imperfections of created human beings who did not chose His first directions.

Jesus is God, Who has controlled history since the beginning. Jesus is not a created being. Jesus was always God. We know this clearly from the Gospel of John: "[1] In the beginning [before all time] was the Word (Christ), and the Word was with God, and the Word was God

Himself. [2] He was [continually existing] in the beginning [co-eternally] with God. [3] All things were made and came into existence through Him; and without Him not even one thing was made that has come into being." (John 1:1-3 AMP) Jesus was there when Satan and other angels fell away from Heaven (Luke 10:18) Jesus already existed when Adam and Eve let Satan trick them into believing a lie. Jesus had chosen to humble Himself and suffer a horrible death experience to pay the sin-debt mankind would generate. Thus He showed the glory of God's love, which He had always experienced. Jesus revealed all of these facts as He prayed with the The Father just before He gave His life as a ransom for everyone: [1] When Jesus had spoken these things, He raised His eyes to heaven [in prayer] and said, "Father, the [a]hour has come. Glorify Your Son, so that Your Son may glorify You. [2] Just as You have given Him power and authority over all mankind, [now glorify Him] so that He may give eternal life [b]to all whom You have given Him [to be His— permanently and forever]. [3] Now this is eternal life: that they may know You, the only true [supreme and sovereign] God, and [in the same manner know] Jesus [as the] Christ whom You have sent. [4] I have glorified You [down here] on the earth by [c]completing the work that You gave Me to do. [5] Now, Father, glorify Me together with Yourself, with the glory and majesty that I had with You before the world existed. (John 17 1-5 AMP). Jesus is the One who has controlled history since the beginning!

Next, we will look at examples of how God controls history in the lives of His people.

*May the peace and love of Christ be with you always!*

# WORDS OF WATER No. 24

"He who believes in Me [who adheres to, trusts in, and relies on Me], as the Scripture has said, 'From his innermost being will flow continually rivers of living water.'" —John 7:38

(For Further Study)

### *Who has controlled history since the beginning?*

Main Texts: Isaiah 41:4; John 1:1-5; Revelation 3:20;
Ephesians 2:8-10; Romans 8:12-15

Now that we know it is God (Father/Son/Spirit) who has controlled history since the beginning, we will look at how Jesus calls each of us to change our history and become part of HIS STORY!

Each of us is born into a family. Some families have a long, rich heritage that they can trace back for centuries. Other families are simply a couple who brought a child into this world. Many families have "histories" of alcoholism, drug abuse, diabetes, poverty, and tribulation. Some families stand upon their wealth and prestige to let everyone know how they have "made it" to the pinnacle of worldly success. But Jesus is calling all people everywhere to break away from those histories. Because no matter how good or bad, healthy or sick, privileged or persecuted you view your history to the point where you meet Jesus, one fact is certain – "all have sinned and continually fall short of the glory of God" (Romans 3:23 AMP) Continuing in your own history without Jesus, regardless of the worldly perspective of that history, is a pathway to hell. You do not have to accept your history however. Jesus says: "[20] Behold, I stand at the door [of the church] and continually knock. If anyone hears My voice and opens the door, I will come in and eat with him (restore him), and he with Me." (Revelation 3:20 AMP)



77

The first step in the changing of history is accepting Jesus. As the Holy Spirit inspired Paul in telling the Ephesians, and all of us: "8 For it is by grace [God's remarkable compassion and favor drawing you to Christ] that you have been saved [actually delivered from judgment and given eternal life] through faith. And this [salvation] is not of yourselves [not through your own effort], but it is the [undeserved, gracious] gift of God; 9 not as a result of [your] works [nor your attempts to keep the Law], so that no one will [be able to] boast or take credit in any way [for his salvation]. 10 For we are His workmanship [His own master work, a work of art], created in Christ Jesus [reborn from above—spiritually transformed, renewed, ready to be used] for good works, which God prepared [for us] beforehand [taking paths which He set], so that we would walk in them [living the good life which He prearranged and made ready for us]. (Ephesians 2:8-10 AMP) God has a new "HIS STORY" to write with us and through us who accept Jesus as Lord and Savior. He wants to mold us all into beautiful works of art – the vessels of His love for others.

The next step is to live out our lives under the guidance of the Holy Spirit. Once we accept salvation, OUR STORY is re-written, and we are going to Heaven as part of HIS STORY. But the devil is still trying to affect the outcome of that history by destroying the works of God.

We need not worry whatsoever because we are part of a new family. We are all part of God's family. We have a different history. We are all capable of living our lives as sons and daughters of God in this new family by the power of the Holy Spirit. Paul explained it like this to the early believers from Rome: "12 So then, brothers and sisters, we have an obligation, but not to our flesh [our human nature, our worldliness, our sinful capacity], to live according to the [impulses of the] flesh [our nature without the Holy Spirit]— 13 for if you are living according to the [impulses of the] flesh, you are going to die. But if [you are living] by the [power of the Holy] Spirit you are habitually putting to death the sinful deeds of the body, you will [really] live forever. [14] For all who are allowing themselves to be led by the Spirit of God are sons of God. [15] For you have not received a spirit of slavery leading again to fear [of God's judgment], but you have received the Spirit of adoption as sons [the Spirit producing sonship] by which we [joyfully] cry, "Abba! Father!" (Romans 8:12-15 AMP)  We can and must reject the lies the devil tries to tell us about who we are based upon our worldly history. The demons have no power over us if we just stand firm against them. God gives us everything we need to live out HIS STORY!

Lastly, we take our place in re-writing history by sharing the good news of Jesus Christ with others. We are commissioned by Jesus to spread His good news (The Gospel). This is our new identity and new purpose. We join with Him in re-writing history: [17] Therefore if anyone is in Christ [that is, grafted in, joined to Him by faith in Him as Savior], he is a new creature [reborn and renewed by the Holy Spirit]; the old things [the previous moral and spiritual condition] have passed away. Behold, new things have come [because spiritual awakening brings a new life]. [18] But all these things are from God, who reconciled us to Himself through Christ [making us acceptable to Him] and gave us the ministry of reconciliation [so that by our example we might bring others to Him], [19] that is, that God was in Christ reconciling the world to Himself, not counting people's sins against them [but canceling them]. And He has committed to us the message of reconciliation [that is, restoration to favor with God]. (Romans 8:12-15). Perhaps you know of someone who's history needs to be re-written?

*May the peace and love of Christ be with you always!*

"He who believes in Me [who adheres to, trusts in, and relies on Me], as the Scripture has said, 'From his innermost being will flow continually rivers of living water.'" —John 7:38

## *God has great plans for you!*

Main Texts: Jerimiah 29:11; Isaiah 30:18 Colossians 1:26-28
John 10:9-11 John 12:24

Is your life going the way you planned it to go?  Are you feeling discouraged?  Are you experiencing panic or anxiety over your circumstances? Maybe you need a new planner. God has great plans for you!  God is always standing by and ready to take over the plans for your life: "¹⁸Therefore  the Lord waits  [expectantly] and longs  to  be gracious to you, And therefore He waits on high to have compassion on you. For the Lord is a God of justice; Blessed (happy, fortunate) are all those who long for Him [since He will never fail them]." (Isaiah 30:18 AMP) He makes it very clear in His Word that He wants to help all of us: "¹¹ For I know the plans and thoughts that I have for you,' says the Lord, 'plans for  peace and well-being  and  not  for disaster, to give you a future and a hope." (Jerimiah 29:11 AMP)



Our God has a great plan for each of us that begins with the hope of eternal life in Heaven. There we will experience eternal well-being and peace, but we do not have to wait until death to begin that plan. The moment we surrender our lives and accept Jesus Christ as our Savior, God's Holy Spirit is given to us and begins the plans that God has made uniquely for each person He created. Paul explained it this way to the early believers in the city of Colosse: "²⁶ that is, the mystery which was hidden [from angels and mankind] for ages and generations, but has now been revealed to His saints (God's people). ²⁷ God [in His eternal plan] chose to make known to them how great for the Gentiles are the riches of the glory of this mystery, which is Christ in and among you, the hope and guarantee of [realizing the] glory. [28] We proclaim Him, warning and instructing everyone in all wisdom [that is, with comprehensive insight into the word and purposes of God], so that we may present every person complete in Christ [mature, fully trained, and perfect in Him—the Anointed]." (Colossians 1:26-28 AMP) God's plan enables everyone to live with Him in Heaven eternally and experience a fulness of life while living on Earth.

We start living by God's plan the moment we accept Jesus as Savior: "[9] I am the Door; anyone who enters through Me will be saved [and will live forever], and will go in and out [freely], and find pasture (spiritual security). [10] The thief comes only in order to steal and kill and destroy. I came that they may have and enjoy life, and have it in abundance [to the full, till it overflows]. (John 10:9-11 AMP) But this means we have to give up our old plans – our old life must "die" much like the fruit of a plant appears to die when it falls to the ground. It separates itself from the old tree or vine, and it starts something new. Jesus described it for us like this: "[24] I assure you and most solemnly say to you, unless a grain of wheat falls into the earth and dies, it remains alone [just one grain, never more]. But if it dies, it produces much grain and yields a harvest. (John 12:24 AMP) Jesus wants to make your life plans for you because He knows the reason He created you. He knows how He plans to help you live a life of joy and peace in the work He has for you in His Kingdom on Earth. He knows that work is going to bless others with His love and bless you in showing His love to others. This is what "the harvest" is all about in the verse above.



There still may be some times of hardship and trials as part of this plan. Jesus' half-brother, James, explained this to the early believers: "[2] Consider it nothing but joy, my brothers and sisters, whenever you fall into various trials. [3] Be assured that the testing of your faith [through experience] produces endurance [leading to spiritual maturity, and inner peace]. ⁴ And let endurance have its perfect result and do a thorough work, so that you may be perfect and completely developed [in your faith], lacking in nothing." (James 1:2-4 AMP)  God's plans for you always provide you with everything you need!

It may not seem like it at the moment, but God knows exactly what He is doing. If you have accepted Jesus Christ as your Savior, God is working out His mavelous plans for you. We should never get discouraged, but build eachother up like it says in the book of Hebrews: "But continually encourage one another every day, as long as it is called "Today" [and there is an opportunity], so that none of you will be hardened [into settled rebellion] by the deceitfulness of sin [its cleverness, delusive glamour, and sophistication]." (Hebrews 3:13 AMP) Look around in the fellowship of believers and encourage someone. And if you are feeling a bit weary along life's journey, always remember these words of Jesus: "²⁷ Peace I leave with you; My [perfect] peace I give to you; not as the world gives do I give to you. Do not let your heart be troubled, nor let it be afraid. [Let My perfect peace calm you in every circumstance and give you courage and strength for every challenge.]" (John 14:27 AMP)  God has great plans for you!

*May the peace and love of Christ be with you always!*

"He who believes in Me [who adheres to, trusts in, and relies on Me], as the Scripture has said, 'From his innermost being will flow continually rivers of living water.'" —John 7:38

## *The Battle Belongs To The Lord!*

Main Texts: 1 Kings 18:18-40; Ephesians 6:11-16; Psalm 23:5-6

Does your life sometimes feel like a battle?  Are you "trying your best" but you feel like your enemies out number you?  Does it seem like you are alone in the fight? The message from this broadcast holds answers for you on how to change the odds and gain the victory. The Battle belongs to the Lord!

We first explore the example of Elijah's "battle" against the false prophets of Baal and Asherah – pagan gods that the Queen Jezebel had promoted within the nation of Israel. She had killed many of the Lord's prophets and Elijah was running for his life. But God revealed Himself to Elijah and told Elijah how to fight the fight differently. In 1 Kings 18:18-40, we can find the entire account. After summoning many people to Mt Carmel, Elijah allows the 450 prophets of Baal, and some 400 prophets of Asherah to place their sacrifice on an alter and call out to their false gods. Nothing happened. "Then Elijah took twelve stones in accordance with the number of the tribes of the sons of Jacob, to whom the word of the Lord had come, saying, "Israel shall be your name." (1 Kings 18;31 AMP). Elijah makes it clear he is doing everything in the name of the Lord – the only true God. And after he allowed his sacrifice to be drenched with water 3 consecutive times he prays: "O Lord, the God of Abraham, Isaac, and Israel (Jacob), let it be known today that You are God in Israel and that I am Your servant and that I have done

> But thanks be to God, which gives us the victory through our Lord Jesus Christ.
>
> —1 Corinthians 15:57

all these things at Your word. [37] Answer me, O Lord, answer me, so that this people may know that You, O Lord, are God, **and that You have turned their hearts back [to You].**" [38] Then the fire of the Lord fell and consumed the burnt offering and the wood, and even the stones and the dust; it also licked up the water in the trench. 39 When all the people saw it, they

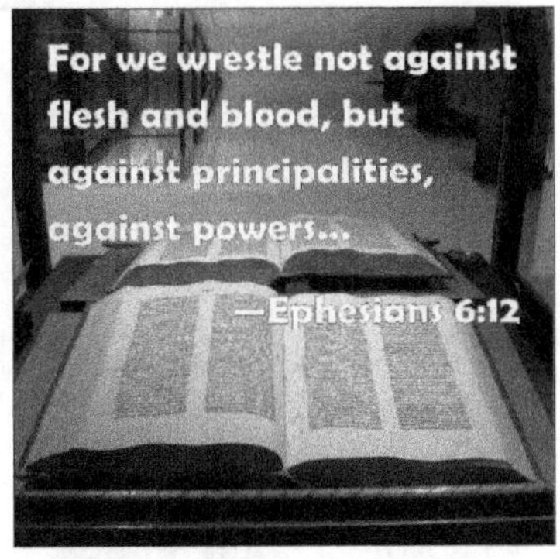


fell face downward; and they said, "The Lord, He is God! The Lord, He is God!" (1 Kings 18:36-39 AMP – emphasis added).

God is always willing to fight the battle for turning hearts towards Himself and away from false gods and idols. He even went as far as sacrificing His own son, Jesus, so that all of our sin debts are paid in full and we can be used to join in that battle. If you have accepted Jesus as Savior, then you must recognize that you are in a different battle, and the battle belongs to the Lord! We now join in the battle to stop the works of the devil and spread the Kingdom of Christ. Paul explained this to the early believers in Ephesus like this: "[11] Put on the full armor of God [for His precepts are like the splendid armor of a heavily-armed soldier], so that you may be able to [successfully] stand up against all the schemes and the strategies and the deceits of the devil. [12] For our struggle is not against flesh and blood [contending only with physical opponents], but against the rulers, against the powers, against the

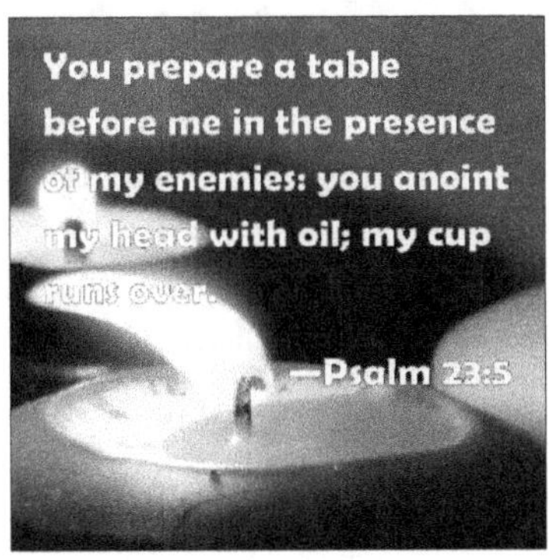


world forces of this [present] darkness, against the spiritual forces of wickedness in the heavenly (supernatural) places. [13] Therefore, put on the complete armor of God, so that you will be able to [successfully] resist and stand your ground in the evil day [of danger], and having done everything [that the crisis demands], to stand firm [in your place, fully prepared, immovable, victorious]." (Ephesians 6:11-13 AMP)

Not only does the battle belong to the Lord, but He also provides us with all the protection and weapons to gain the victory! We can protect our minds and thoughts by remembering we are saved by faith through grace. Our hearts, our innermost being is protected because we have the righteousness of Christ covering us.

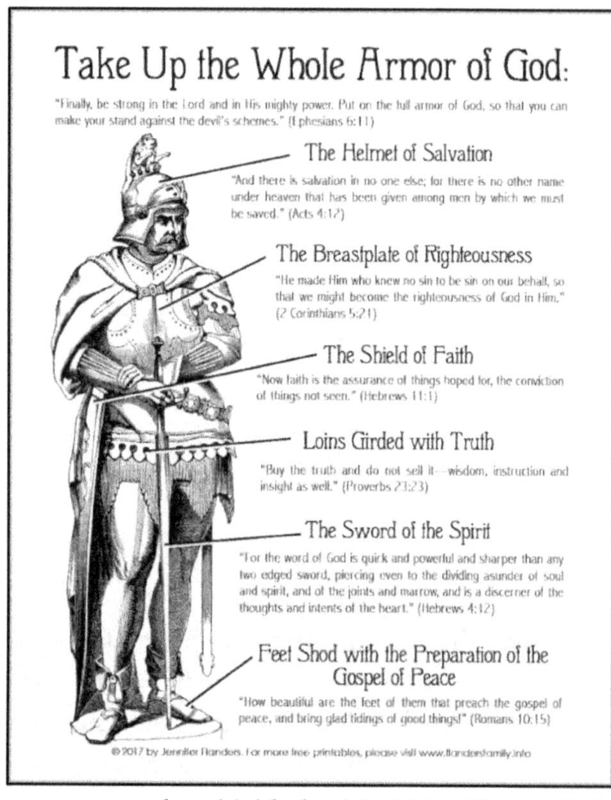



Any attacks from the enemy can be shielded with faith. We are held together tightly with a belt of real truth — we know God loves us and will never leave us or forsake us. We walk out our lives knowing that the good news of the Gospel will never wear out. And we are given an amazing weapon, the Holy Spirit power of the Words of God! And as God promised through the prophet Isaiah: "No weapon that is formed against you will succeed; And every tongue that rises against you in judgment you will condemn. This [peace, righteousness, security, and triumph over opposition] is the heritage of the servants of the Lord, And this is their vindication from Me," says the Lord. (Isaiah 54:16-17 AMP)

We have no reason to be anxious about any battle we face. We need only to make sure that we are equipping ourselves properly and following the Lord's directions. When we do that, we can stand firmly against the enemies of our lives and enjoy the same experience that King David depicted in his famous Psalm 23:

[5] You prepare a table before me in the presence of my enemies.
You have anointed and refreshed my head with oil;
My cup overflows.
[6] Surely goodness and mercy and unfailing love shall follow me all the
days of my life,
And I shall dwell forever [throughout all my days] in the house and in
the presence of the Lord.
(Psalm 23:5-6 AMP)

*May the peace and love of Christ be with you always!*

"He who believes in Me [who adheres to, trusts in, and relies on Me], as the Scripture has said, 'From his innermost being will flow continually rivers of living water.'" —John 7:38

## *Walking Into The Favor Of God*

Main Texts: Hebrews 11:1-6; John 15:6-8; Galatians 5:22-23

Remember back to when your parents were taking care of you? You listened to what they told you. You trusted that what they were telling you was for your own good, and so you obeyed whatever they told you to do. Life just worked. That special thing you wanted and mentioned in passing at the dinner table "magically" showed up at a birthday or Christmas. Both you and your parents were happy.

Then you got older. You started to question what your parents told you. You started trying things you knew they may not approve of and life started getting harder. Maybe relations got tense with your parents? Suddenly, you were "learning lessons" and things just seemed to be more difficult. God gave people these experiences so they could relate to Him better when they grew old enough to be adults. We can choose to "do things our way" or walk into the favor of God!

Let's look at how God's favor works. First and foremost, we must accept Jesus as Lord and Savior of our life. We must believe in our hearts that Jesus paid our sin debt in full and has redeemed our lives for eternity. We must believe He has our best in mind, similar to what we thought of our parents when we were small children. Once we receive His gift of salvation, we can exercise our FAITH.

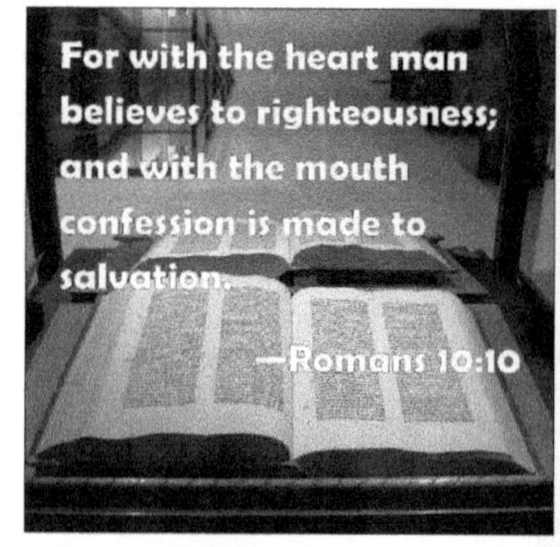


Hebrews 11:1 AMP defines faith: "Now faith is the assurance (title deed, confirmation) of things hoped for (divinely guaranteed), and the evidence of things not seen [the conviction of their reality—faith

comprehends as fact what cannot be experienced by the physical senses].” When we put our faith to the test, we must LISTEN /TRUST /and OBEY what Jesus (the Holy Spirit) is prompting us to do. A great example of this is found in John's Gospel, the ninth chapter. Jesus and the disciples come upon a blind man. The disciples ask Jesus about why the man was blind from birth.

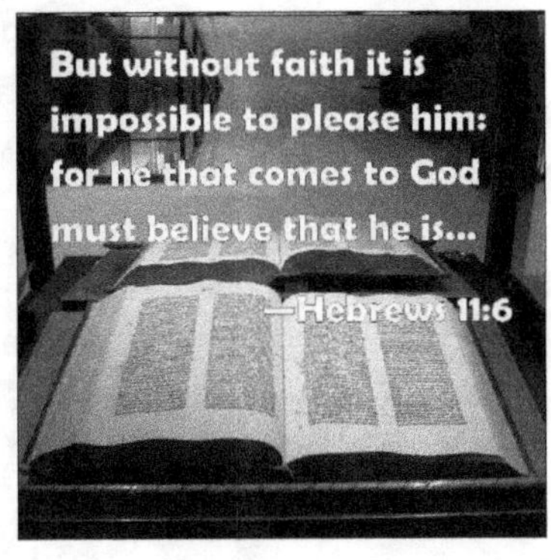


Jesus replies, "Neither this man nor his parents sinned, but it was so that the works of God might be displayed and illustrated in him." John 9:3 AMP) To operate within God's favor, we must be in line with God's will and purpose. Often, we will not see the "logic" of what God is doing, but we LISTEN /TRUST/ and OBEY in faith. Jesus could have just spoke or touched the man and given him his sight. But Jesus makes mud out of dirt and His own saliva. He puts it on the man's eyes and tells him to go and wash in the pool of Siloam. Not exactly sanitary procedures, right? The man could have sat there and reasoned with Jesus about "the best approach" to his situation. But the man did not question Jesus' techniques or methods, he just LISTENED /TRUSTED/ and OBEYED. The result was that not only did the man receive his sight, but many other people at the pool got to witness to the miracle. God's glory was multiplied!

Jesus invites all of us to walk into the favor of God. Here is how He explained it for us: "⁷ If you remain in Me and My words remain in you [that is, if we are vitally united and My message lives in your heart], ask whatever you wish and it will be done for you. ⁸ My Father is glorified and honored by this, when you bear much fruit, and prove yourselves to be My [true] disciples. (John 15:6-8 AMP)

Look very closely at the verses above. Jesus saiys we should be connected to Him in a vital way – meaning extremely important. His message is alive in our hearts – it is or has become part of our personality. We are in complete obedience to what Jesus has demonstrated. We are humbled and open to the promptings of the Holy

Spirit. We are not just hearers of the Word, but we act upon what we hear because we trust that God is working all things for good. (James 1:22 / Romans 8:28). And the fruits resulting from our work glorifies to God: [22] But the fruit of the Spirit [the result of His presence within us] is love [unselfish concern for others], joy, [inner] peace, patience [not the ability to wait, but how we act while waiting], kindness, goodness, faithfulness, [23] gentleness, self-control. Against such things there is no law. (Galatians 5:22-23 AMP) When we stay connected to Jesus, we walk into the favor of God by faith and do works that yield wonderful fruit. If you are tired of doing life your way, humble yourself and accept the connection to Jesus. Then walk into the favor of God!

*May the peace and love of Christ be with you always!*

"He who believes in Me [who adheres to, trusts in, and relies on Me], as the Scripture has said, 'From his innermost being will flow continually rivers of living water.'" —John 7:38

## *Is God Pleased With Your Offering & Sacrifice?*

Main Texts: Genesis 4:1-5; Acts 5:1-5; Ezekiel 37:5

In this message, Offering and Sacrifice are lumped together and include the Tithe, free will offerings, and voluntary (votive) offerings, meaning time/talent/treasure that we say we will give to God. The reason these are being lumped together is because we are looking at this topic from God's perspective. Since He supplies everything we have, including the air we breathe, the water we drink, the food we eat, He looks at our hearts – the attitude and mindset - when we are giving back to Him these offerings and sacrifices. Last week, we explored walking into God's favor, and this is a continuation of that message. If we hope to walk in God's favor, then we must have **FAITH** in what pleases God and act out of obedience and humility.



God gives us everything we need – period. He does this from His endless attitude and mindset of love. Even though we have all sinned and deserve eternal punishment, God gives us salvation: "For God so [greatly] loved and dearly prized the world, that He [even] gave His [One and] only begotten Son, so that whoever believes and trusts in Him [as Savior] shall not perish, but have eternal life." (John 3:16 AMP) When we stand upon this truth in faith, we cannot help but want to be in obedience and offer back with a heart of thanksgiving and praise. God always gives us first, and it pleases Him when we give back with a heart of humility and faith. This has been His way from the very beginning.

In the very early chapters of Genesis, we see this insight into what pleases God. Even though Adam and Eve had disobeyed God, and were expelled from Eden, God continued to bless them and provide for them.

In the account of Cain and Abel, the first of Eve's sons after the fall, we see clearly how God views offerings: [3]"And in the course of time Cain brought to the Lord an offering of the fruit of the ground. [4] But Abel brought [an offering of] the [finest] firstborn of his flock and the fat portions. And the Lord had respect (regard) for Abel and for his offering; [5] but for Cain and his offering He had no respect. So Cain became extremely angry (indignant), and he looked annoyed and hostile. [6] And the Lord said to Cain, "Why are you so angry? And why do you look annoyed? [7] If you do well [believing Me and doing what is acceptable and pleasing to Me], will you not be accepted? And if you do not do well [but ignore My instruction], sin crouches at your door; its desire is for you [to overpower you], but you must master it." (Genesis 4:3-7 AMP)

Abel took great care in preparing his best possessions for an offering (back) to God, but Cain simply threw together some of his left overs. Cain was frustrated with God because Cain did not grasp God's power to protect Cain and give him favor over sinfulness. In effect, God was offering a second chance to the sons of Eve, but instead of humbling himself before God, and doing what pleased God, Cain killed Abel out of jealousy!  This started an entire legacy of sinfulness in Cain's descendants (see Genesis 4, onward from the 9th verse). But God was not done providing. God gave Eve a third son, "[25] Adam knew [Eve as] his wife again; and she gave birth to a son, and named him Seth, for [she said], "God has granted another child for me in place of Abel, because Cain killed him." [26] To Seth, also, a son was born, whom he named Enosh (mortal man, mankind). At that [same] time men began to call on the name of the Lord [in worship through prayer, praise, and thanksgiving]. (Genesis 4:25-26) From that lineage would come Noah (Genesis 5), Abraham, David, and eventually Jesus! (Mathew 1). Is God pleased with your offerings and sacrifice?

We next look at an example from the New Testament. In the early Church, many believers of means were making significant contributions so that those in need had provisions and the Kingdom message (expanding the Church) was supported. But here again, God gives us the warning to be sure we are giving (back) to Him with a proper heart:  ¹Now a man named Ananias, with his wife Sapphira, sold a piece of property, ² and with his wife's full knowledge [and complicity] he kept back some of the proceeds, bringing only a portion of it, and set it at the apostles' feet. ³ But Peter said, "Ananias, why has Satan filled your heart to lie to the Holy Spirit and [secretly] keep back for yourself some of the proceeds [from the sale] of the land? ⁴ As long as it remained [unsold], did it not remain your own [to do with as you pleased]? And after it was sold, was the money not under your control? Why is it that you have conceived this act [of hypocrisy and deceit] in your heart? You have not [simply] lied to people, but to God." ⁵ And hearing these words, Ananias fell down suddenly and died; and great fear and awe gripped those who heard of it. (Acts 5:1-5 AMP)

Later, Sapphira experienced the same outcome!  Clearly it was not about the amount they were giving but about the attitude and mindset. These two were not giving out of humility, gratitude, and obedience. They were trying to put on an outward appearance and being deceitful to their fellow believers and to God Himself. God does not need anything. If he wants to, He can take dead, dry bones and return them to living beings! God is simply looking at our attitude, mindset and obedience – our **FAITH** – as we offer back and make sacrifices of our time/talents/treasures. Is God pleased with your offerings and sacrifice?

*May the peace and love of Christ be with you always!*

"He who believes in Me [who adheres to, trusts in, and relies on Me], as the Scripture has said, 'From his innermost being will flow continually rivers of living water.'" —John 7:38

(For Further Study)
### *Is God Pleased With Your Offering & Sacrifice?*

Main Texts: Malachi 3:7-12; Acts 2:44-45; Philippians 4:12-20

We are going deeper into this message because it is so important on so many levels. Ever wonder why there is a scarcity mentality among individual Christians and the Church overall?  If we listen closely, it almost sounds like the children of God are "begging" for support. This is exactly the opposite of God's intentions and what pleases God. Think about it for a second:



1. God created and controls everything – so He needs nothing
2. God expects His believers to use what He supplies to some in abundance to bless those in temporary want until they, too, can bless out of abundance. (Leviticus 27)
3. As others see the mutual love and support of believers, they become curious about this supernatural love and abundance and the Holy Spirit calls them to believe.
4. But God is also perfectly just, so if His people do not follow His commandments (to love God and love others as themselves) He must deliver consequences.

This has always been "God's ways" as we saw last time from Genesis 4 and the story of Cain and Able. We not only dis-please God when we fail to exercise our **FAITH** and pretend like our time/ talents/ and treasures belong solely to ourselves, we are also actually stealing from the economy that God designed!  God makes this very clear: [7] "Yet from the days of your fathers you have turned away from My statutes and ordinances and have not kept them. Return to Me, and I will return to you," says the Lord of hosts. "But you say, 'How shall we return?'[8] "Will a man rob God? Yet you are robbing Me! But you say, 'In what way have we robbed You?' In

tithes and offerings [you have withheld]. [9] You are cursed with a curse, for you are robbing Me, this whole nation! [10] Bring all the tithes (the tenth) into the storehouse, so that there may be food in My house, and test Me now in this," says the Lord of hosts, "if I will not open for you the windows of heaven and pour out for you [so great] a blessing until there is no more room to receive it. [11] Then I will rebuke the devourer (insects, plague) for your sake and he will not destroy the fruits of the ground, nor will your vine in the field drop its grapes [before harvest]," says the Lord of hosts. [12] "All nations shall call you happy and blessed, for you shall be a land of delight," says the Lord of hosts. (Malachi 3:7-12 AMP)  Amazing is it not; the God of the Universe is actually challenging His creation to be faithful — all anyone needs to do is believe — have enough **FAITH** to take God at His Words! Is God pleased with your offerings and sacrifice?

Have any of us ever wondered why Jesus never gave a sermon or teaching around donating to His ministry?  He talked a lot about how to be a good steward of money, but we have no record of Him ending a

sermon or preaching with a request for a donation! We know He recruited some fishermen, and one tax collector as disciples. We are told in Luke 8 that several wealthy women supported the ministry. He also sent His disciples into the nearby towns and villages in Mark 6, but He told them to take no provisions. Jesus fully expected provision because He

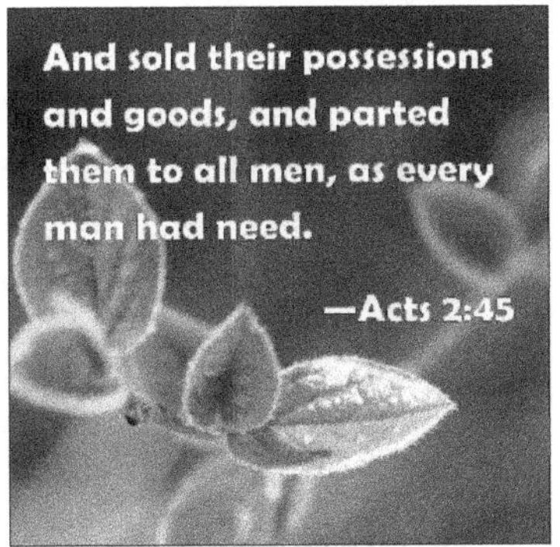

had perfect faith. And this was the heart of the earliest believers: ""44 And all those who had believed [in Jesus as Savior] were together and had all things in common [considering their possessions to belong to the group as a whole]. 45 And they began selling their property and possessions and were sharing the proceeds with all [the other believers], as anyone had need." (Acts 2:44-45 AMP)  We learned last time what happened to Ananias and Sapphira when they tried to hold back what they had committed to God (Acts 5:1-10). Is God pleased with your offerings and sacrifice?

Lastly, let's look at the example of the Apostle Paul. In writing to the early Church in Philippi he says: ""12 I know how to get along and live humbly [in difficult times], and I also know how to enjoy abundance and live in prosperity. In any and every circumstance I have learned the secret [of facing life], whether well-fed or going hungry, whether having an abundance or being in need. 13 I can do all things [which He has called me to do] through Him who strengthens and empowers me [to fulfill His purpose—I am self-sufficient in Christ's sufficiency; I am ready for anything and equal to anything through Him who infuses me with inner strength and confident peace.] 14 Nevertheless, it was right of you to share [with me] in my difficulties.

15 And you Philippians know that in the early days of preaching the gospel, after I left Macedonia, no church shared with me in the matter of giving and receiving except you alone; 16 for even in Thessalonica you sent a gift more than once for my needs. 17 Not that I seek the gift itself, but I do seek the profit which increases to your [heavenly] account [the

blessing which is accumulating for you]. 18 But I have received everything in full and more; I am amply supplied, having received from Epaphroditus the gifts you sent me. They are the fragrant aroma of an offering, an acceptable sacrifice which God welcomes and in which He delights. 19 And my God will liberally supply (fill until full) your every need according to His riches in glory in Christ Jesus. [20] To our God and Father be the glory forever and ever. Amen" (Philippians 4:12-20 AMP) Paul was not just thanking them for a donation. Paul was reminding them how God's economy is designed. Paul was reminding them (and each of us) that God delights in the acceptable sacrifices – ones where His believers are trusting Him for spiritual power and material replenishment; and having **FAITH** that in their blessing of others, they will receive a blessing. Is God pleased with your offerings and sacrifice?

*May the peace and love of Christ be with you always*

"He who believes in Me [who adheres to, trusts in, and relies on Me], as the Scripture has said, 'From his innermost being will flow continually rivers of living water.'" —John 7:38

## *Stand up on your feet*

Main Texts: John 12:46-47; Ezekiel 2:1, 8; Ephesians 6:11-12; Isaiah 60:1-2; Luke 10:19

This broadcast was the third in the series on "Walking Into The Favor of God," started on September 20, 2020. This broadcast focused on "Stand Up On Your Feet" because one cannot walk into the favor of God unless one is standing! So first, we must understand what gives us the ability to stand up in the first place.

It always begins with Jesus! If we have not accepted our free gift of salvation by grace through faith, we sit in the darkness and have no hope. Jesus told us clearly: "[46] I have come as Light into the world, so that everyone who believes and trusts in Me [as Savior—all those who anchor their hope in Me and rely on the truth of My message] will not continue to live in

darkness. [47] If anyone hears My words and does not keep them, I do not judge him; for I did not come to judge and condemn the world [that is, to initiate the final judgment of the world], but to save the world. (John 12:46-47 AMP) If we want to stand on our feet and walk into the favor of God, we must have Jesus as our Savior and Lord! We can stand, but only in His light.

Standing is a symbolic posture. In the military, soldiers "stand at attention" whenever a person of rank is speaking to them. Likewise, God expects our respect and worship, so throughout the Bible, He requires humans to stand up for instruction and favor. One great example is the Prophet Ezekiel: "Then He said to me, "Son of man, stand on your feet and I will speak to you. [2] Then as He spoke to me the Spirit entered me and set me on my feet; and I heard Him speaking to me." (Ezekiel 2:1-2 AMP)  In this case, the Holy Spirt actually stood Ezekiel on to his feet!  God wanted to impart a significant message for the people of Israel into Ezekiel and He required him to stand on his feet!

Standing up, when you analyze it closely, is literally the first step of walking. You cannot walk sitting down. You cannot walk into the favor of God sitting down either. God wants us to stand up against the forces of evil and not be afraid. Look at how Paul explained it to the early believers in Ephesus: "[11] Put on the full armor of God [for His precepts are like the splendid armor of a heavily-armed soldier], so that you may be able to [successfully] stand up against all the schemes and the strategies and the deceits of the devil. [12] For our struggle is not against flesh and blood [contending only with physical opponents], but against the rulers, against the powers, against the world forces of this [present] darkness, against the spiritual forces of wickedness in the heavenly (supernatural) places. (Ephesians 6:11-12 AMP) Spiritually, we must all stand up, stand firm, and then walk into the favor of God!

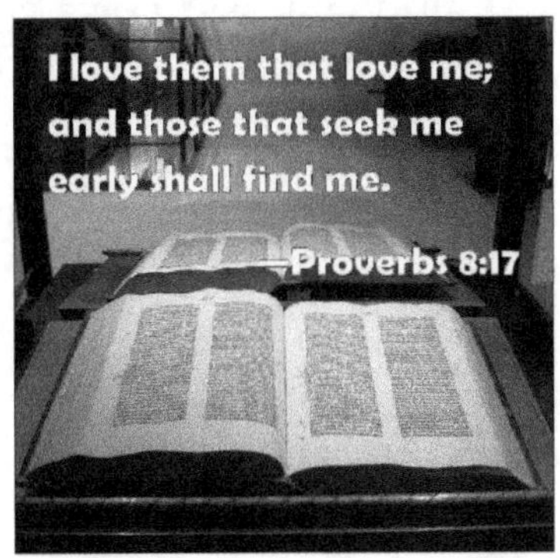


So, we know that Christ illuminates our lives and invites us to stand up to put on our full armor,  God promises that when we do, supernatural favor awaits us: [1]"Arise [from spiritual depression to a new life], shine [be radiant with the glory and brilliance of the Lord]; for your light has come, And the glory and brilliance of the Lord has risen upon you.[2] "For in fact, darkness will cover the earthAnd deep darkness will cover the peoples; But the Lord will rise upon you [Jerusalem] And His glory and brilliance will be seen on you.[3] "Nations will come to your light, And kings to the brightness of your rising." (Isaiah 60:1-3 AMP) And Jesus said to the disciples: [19] "Listen carefully: I have given you authority [that you now possess] to tread on serpents and scorpions, and [the ability to exercise authority] over all the power of the enemy

(Satan); and nothing will [in any way] harm you. [20] Nevertheless do not rejoice at this, that the spirits are subject to you, but rejoice that your names are recorded in heaven." (Luke10:19-20 AMP) We have everything we need if we just stand up on our feet!

Finally, God gives us specific instructions on how we should walk if we want to walk into His favor: [15] "Therefore see that you walk carefully [living life with honor, purpose, and courage; shunning those who tolerate and enable evil], not as the unwise, but as wise [sensible, intelligent, discerning people], [16] making the very most of your time [on earth, recognizing and taking advantage of each opportunity and using it with wisdom and diligence], because the days are [filled with] evil. [17] Therefore do not be foolish and thoughtless, but understand and firmly grasp what the will of the Lord is. [18] Do not get drunk with wine, for that is wickedness (corruption, stupidity), but be filled with the [Holy] Spirit and constantly guided by Him. (Ephesians 5:15-18 AMP) We stand on our feet to receive the light of Christ and put on His full armor, and then we walk in His light, directed by the Holy Spirit, so that we may experience the favor of God that awaits us daily.

*May the peace and love of Christ be with you always*

"He who believes in Me [who adheres to, trusts in, and relies on Me], as the Scripture has said, 'From his innermost being will flow continually rivers of living water.'" —John 7:38

### *I am blessed in the Lord's Name!*

Main Texts: John 12:46-47; Ezekiel 2:1, 8; Ephesians 6:11-12;

God's original intent was to have mankind (men and women) steward His creation and share in a loving relationship with God (Father/Son/Spirit). He did not create them as gods, but He did bless them and provide them a status above all the rest of creation. God gave them everything they needed to fulfill His plans, and only one limitation:

"[28] And God blessed them [granting them certain authority] and said to them, "Be fruitful, multiply, and fill the earth, and subjugate it [putting it under your power]; and rule over (dominate) the fish of the sea, the birds of the air, and every living thing that moves upon the earth." [29] So God said, "Behold, I have given you every plant yielding seed that is on the surface of the entire earth, and every tree which has fruit yielding seed; it shall be food for you; [30] and to all the animals on the earth and to every bird of the air and to everything that moves on the ground—to everything in which there is the breath of life—I have given every green plant for food"; and it was so [because He commanded it]. [31] God saw everything that He had made, and behold, it was very good and He validated it completely. And there was evening and there was morning, a sixth day.// [15] So the LORD God took the man [He had made] and settled him in the Garden of Eden to cultivate and keep it. [16] And the LORD God commanded the man, saying, "You may freely (unconditionally) eat [the fruit] from every tree of the garden; [17] but [only] from the tree of the knowledge (recognition) of good and evil you shall not eat, otherwise on the day that you eat from it, you shall most certainly [b]die [because of your disobedience]." (Genesis 1:28-31; and 2:17-17 AMP) Mankind was not obedient, however, and disobeyed this one command that God had given in order that mankind could freely love the Creator.

Thankfully, this is only the beginning of the story about the God who's Name is above all names!  In fact, God began a redemptive work from that moment because nothing can stand in the way of God's will. God told Moses about His reasoning when He was preparing Moses to talk to the Pharaoh of Egypt: "[15] For by now I could have put out My hand and struck you and your people with a pestilence, and you would then have been cut off (obliterated) from the earth. [16] But indeed for this very reason I have allowed you to live, in order to show you My power and in order that My name may be proclaimed throughout all the earth. (Exodus 9:15-16 AMP) God's intent to glorify the Trinity through creation, and to enjoy a loving relationship with mankind is made possible again through the sin-debt paid by Jesus on the cross:

**[14] Just as Moses lifted up the [bronze] serpent in the desert [on a pole], so must the Son of Man be lifted up [on the cross], [15] so that whoever believes will in Him have eternal life [after physical death, and will actually live forever]. [16] "For God so [greatly] loved and dearly prized the world, that He [even] gave His [One and] only begotten Son, so that whoever believes and trusts in Him [as Savior] shall not perish, but have eternal life. [17] For God did not send the Son into the world to judge and condemn the world [that is, to initiate the final judgment of the world], but that the world might be saved through Him. [18] Whoever believes and has decided to trust in Him [as personal Savior and Lord] is not judged [for this one, there is no judgment, no rejection, no condemnation]; but the one who does not believe [and has decided to reject Him as personal Savior and Lord] is judged already [that one has been convicted and sentenced], because he has not believed and trusted in the name of the [One and] only begotten Son of God [the One who is truly unique, the only One of His kind, the One who alone can save**

**him].** (John 3:14-18 AMP- highlighting added) **There is only one name through which you are blessed – that name is Jesus!**

Now that we have this salvation through faith by grace, we can, once again, know we are blessed to fulfill the original plan God has for us. We need to shake off the lies of the evil forces in this world and "take dominion." We need to know that we are God's children and He longs to favor us! We need to shine as examples of hope in this dark world. Paul explained it clearly to the early believers in Philippi:

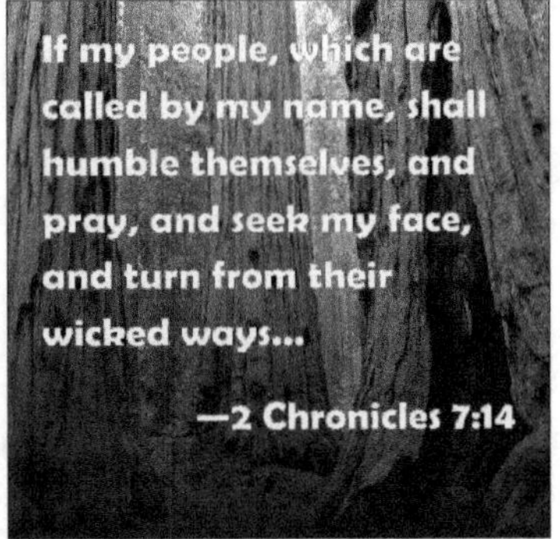


"¹⁴ Do everything without murmuring or questioning [the providence of God], ¹⁵ so that you may prove yourselves to be blameless and guileless, innocent and uncontaminated, children of God without blemish in the midst of a [morally] crooked and [spiritually] perverted generation, among whom you are seen as bright lights [beacons shining out clearly] in the world [of darkness], ¹⁶ holding out and offering to everyone the word of life, so that in the day of Christ I will have reason to rejoice greatly because I did not run [my race] in vain nor labor without result. (Philippians 2:14-16 AMP)

*Does the way you live tell everyone, "I am blessed in the Lord's Name"?*

*May the peace and love of Christ be with you always!*

# Chapter Video Links

1. https://www.facebook.com/watch/live/?v=6242660284443609&ref=watch_permalink
2. https://www.facebook.com/watch/live/?v=6242660284443609&ref=watch_permalink
3. https://www.facebook.com/watch/live/?v=2936565256444141&ref=watch_permalink
4. https://www.facebook.com/watch/live/?v=8147098956000151&ref=watch_permalink
5. https://www.facebook.com/watch/live/?v=8147098956000151&ref=watch_permalink
6. https://www.facebook.com/watch/live/?v=2657015684399726&ref=watch_permalink
7. https://www.facebook.com/watch/live/?v=2657015684399726&ref=watch_permalink
8. https://www.facebook.com/yaw.a.amankwah/videos/10158937151447780/UzpfSTQ5NTk4MDU0NzIwODA4NToxNzg3NzYzMDQ4MDI5ODIy/
9. https://www.facebook.com/yaw.a.amankwah/videos/10158937151447780/UzpfSTQ5NTk4MDU0NzIwODA4NToxNzg3NzYzMDQ4MDI5ODIy/
10. https://www.facebook.com/watch/live/?v=7062079993555789&ref=watch_permalink
11. https://www.facebook.com/watch/live/?v=7062079993555789&ref=watch_permalink
12. https://www.facebook.com/watch/live/?v=7062079993555789&ref=watch_permalink
13. https://www.facebook.com/watch/live/?v=2111075869997122&ref=watch_permalink
14. https://www.facebook.com/watch/live/?v=2111075869997122&ref=watch_permalink
15. https://www.facebook.com/watch/live/?v=9502727087780142&ref=watch_permalink

16. https://www.facebook.com/watch/live/?v=9502727087801 42&ref=watch_permalink
17. https://www.facebook.com/watch/live/?v=9502727087801 42&ref=watch_permalink
18. https://www.facebook.com/watch/live/?v=2935609485421 86&ref=watch_permalink
19. https://www.facebook.com/watch/live/?v=1643278185852299&ref=watch_permalink
20. https://www.facebook.com/watch/live/?v=1643278185852299&ref=watch_permalink
21. https://www.facebook.com/watch/live/?v=5326460475039 95&ref=watch_permalink
22. https://www.facebook.com/watch/live/?v=5326460475039 95&ref=watch_permalink
23. https://www.facebook.com/watch/live/?v=3835444793095 10&ref=watch_permalink
24. https://www.facebook.com/watch/live/?v=3835444793095 10&ref=watch_permalink
25. https://www.facebook.com/watch/live/?v=3301392149741 81&ref=watch_permalink
26. https://www.facebook.com/watch/live/?v=3726990553980598&ref=watch_permalink
27. https://www.facebook.com/watch/live/?v=4060427603877 57&ref=watch_permalink
28. https://www.facebook.com/watch/live/?v=8746715830640 65&ref=watch_permalink
29. https://www.facebook.com/watch/live/?v=8746715830640 65&ref=watch_permalink
30. https://www.facebook.com/watch/live/?v=1482440951965122&ref=watch_permalink
31. https://www.facebook.com/watch/live/?v=2936565256444141&ref=watch_permalink